HOPE

UNCOMMON LEADERSHIP

SERVANT LEADERSHIP IN A POWER-BASED WORLD

ROBERT D. KUEST

Hope International University Press
Fullerton, CA

© 2006 by Robert Kuest. All rights reserved.

Pleasant Word (a division of WinePress Publishing, PO Box 428, Enumclaw, WA 98022) functions only as book publisher. As such, the ultimate design, content, editorial accuracy, and views expressed or implied in this work are those of the author.

Hope International University Press
2500 E. Nutwood Avenue
Fullerton, CA 90831

No part of this publication may be reproduced, stored in a retrieval system or transmitted in any way by any means—electronic, mechanical, photocopy, recording or otherwise—without the prior permission of the copyright holder, except as provided by USA copyright law.

Unless otherwise noted, all Scriptures are taken from the Holy Bible, New International Version, Copyright © 1973, 1978, 1984 by the International Bible Society. Used by permission of Zondervan Publishing House. The "NIV" and "New International Version" trademarks are registered in the United States Patent and Trademark Office by International Bible Society.

ISBN 1-4141-0459-6
Library of Congress Catalog Card Number: 2005925533

ATTESTATIONS

Bob Kuest has touched upon an approach to leadership that is both biblical and practical. His concepts are well stated and documented. The style of writing is easily understood, but has great depth. I highly recommend his book to leaders in all cultures and areas of service.

—Joe Grana, Ph.D.
Christian Ministries Department Head
Hope International University
Fullerton, CA

This book is a must read for all those who are hungry to lead God's people the right way. In this book Bob draws our attention to one of the most critical issues in how to be a servant leader as Jesus was. This book is prophetic to the church leadership in Africa, and in tune with the times, while being faithful to Scripture. It is thoughtfully upbeat, practical and brave.

> —Emmanuel Zihove, Church Planter and
> Director of Community Bible Studies
> International for Southern Africa
> Harare, Zimbabwe

This is not a common book. I have read many books on leadership but none like this book. It is easy to understand and to apply in every culture. Dr. Bob Kuest put the biblical leadership principles in a way that can be understood by every Christian in every corner of the world, regardless of education level. He has held seminars in Thailand every year since 1999. People are still asking for more. There are good reasons behind it: biblical truth, cultural understanding, and experience with God's Kingdom in different countries around the world. This is the book for today's church leaders for their future ministry.

> Ahtapa Sinlee, Founder/Director
> Asian Gospel Outreach
> Pamadang, Thailand

DEDICATION

To Peggy,
My wife, partner, and best friend.
She has supported and encouraged me
through all the ups and down of ministry.

TABLE OF CONTENTS

Foreword xi
Acknowledgements xv
Introduction xix

Chapter One: Uncommon Thinking 25
Chapter Two: Uncommon Measurements 43
Chapter Three: Uncommon Purpose 65
Chapter Four: Uncommon Paradigm 79
Chapter Five: Uncommon Strategy 93
Chapter Six: Uncommon Testing 105
Chapter Seven: Uncommon Authority 125
Chapter Eight: Jesus – An Incarnational
    Leader 153
Chapter Nine: David – Ruler in
    Righteousness 167
Chapter Ten: Paul – Builder of People 181

Chapter Eleven: Uncommon Courage 199

Epilogue 217

Appendix A: A Comparison of Plato's
   Philosophy vs. Theology Revealed
   through Moses..221
Appendix B: Leadership Styles Chart................223
Appendix C: Translation Comparisons
   of Words Used for Leadership 227
Appendix D: A New Testament Word
   Study Leadership & Authority 231
Appendix E: Descending to Serve 235

Source List...239
Endnotes 245

FOREWORD

A few years ago I was in Africa with Bob and Peggy Kuest. They were the honored guests, teaching on leadership and what it means to be called a leader. Many of the pastors and church leaders were from remote rural areas and needed to meet with the local hosts after dinner one night. After a long day of teaching, the Kuests were sent off to rest while the local pastors and leaders were meeting.

I next saw Bob and Peggy cleaning the pots and pans, washing dishes and sweeping up while the children giggled nervously at such a counter-cultural action. When the meetings finished the women saw that the work they were expecting to be waiting on them had been completed. They were scandalized that such high status people would do such menial tasks, but they were also grateful for the help.

This life of service is what makes Bob qualified to write a book on leadership. Bob and Peggy exemplify the biblical definition of servant leader—never grasping, never holding on to position, but serving others as if they were serving the Lord Himself. In Uncommon Leadership Bob shows how servant leadership is not just a catch phrase but the very core of what God intended a leader to demonstrate.

The first time I became aware of leadership as an academic discipline was when my wife and I returned from Kenya and were trying to discern God's will for our future. Several of the elders in the church where the Kuests were ministers were helping me to pray and think through the process. Ken and Jim showed me a lesson on leadership Bob had been teaching them and made application to my life and situation. That conversation clarified for me that I needed to accept the role of leadership God was calling me into. Furthermore, my full potential would only be realized if I followed biblical patterns of leadership.

I am still trying to apply the principles Bob has laid out in *Uncommon Leadership*. The Bible should be our guide, as he points out, rather than business models. Yes, we can learn from business models, and we should understand them, but the standard is what God has shown us through His Word. This is indeed uncommon leadership.

I was pleased when the Kuests joined NMSI in 1998 and brought their wisdom into our growing mission agency. They have taught in Central and

Foreword

North America, Africa, Europe and Asia since that time to thousands of church leaders. I have heard testimonies of many church leaders whose lives and ministries have been transformed by application of the principles taught by Bob and Peggy.

I know that *Uncommon Leadership* will be used to extend the reach of the Kuests' ministry even beyond where they can go. Written in a style to allow it to be used by pastors and church leaders in seminars and courses globally, this is a valuable asset to the body of resources available to non-North American church leaders.

Uncommon Leadership is not just for the newly emerging church, but should be read by every pastor, elder and aspiring church leader in North America. Our power based models of leadership are so deeply a part of our cultural and religious context that most of us do not even realize how far from God's plan of leadership we have strayed. The established church needs this book. My prayer is that biblical leadership in coming generations will no longer be "uncommon."

—Phil Hudson, President
New Mission Systems International

ACKNOWLEDGEMENTS

As I contemplate the writing of this book I think back to those who have contributed in so many ways. I have come to believe that it would be nearly impossible for an individual to write a book and take sole credit for it. Therefore, I desire to thank God for those He has sent to be my team.

This book would not be possible without the love and support of my wife, Peggy, who has encouraged me through times when thoughts flowed freely and times when I was ready to throw the whole project out the window. We have always traveled as a team and even though she has heard these concepts over and over, she still sits in on every session to be my prayer partner and cheerleader. I am the one who has been blessed since the day she walked into my life.

God has blessed us with four wonderful children – Dean, David, Sheila and Scott. The last chapter of this book was written by our oldest son, Dean. He is a pastor and an avid student of leadership. He has contributed ideas and reading suggestions that have helped to keep me current. As explained in the introduction to his chapter, his rising to the occasion to deliver this message on September 13, 2001, made his mom and me very proud.

I want to thank my friend and colleague, Dr. Dan Denton, who kept saying to me, "Bob, you have to write this. It would be wrong for you to not do so." Over many lunchtime discussions he encouraged me to "get it done." Well, Dan, here it is.

I want to thank Mike and Delores Hines, friends since the mid-70s, who have traveled and taught with us. Mike has always been an excellent person to bounce around ideas and to help me keep them true to Scripture. I always enjoy our stimulating "one-on-one" discussions. He and Delores proofread this manuscript and offered excellent suggestions. Thanks to both of you for friendship and help.

Dr. Tamsen Murray, a friend and fellow Professor of Leadership, has been a believer in our ministry from its very start and a dear friend to my wife. She helped me with writing style and held me accountable by always asking, "What is your source?"

Acknowledgements

I am grateful to Dr. Joe Grana for his encouragement to write and willingness to read my manuscript and offer guidance.

Phil Hudson is the President of New Mission Systems International and my mentor in missions. I have learned so much from him on understanding worldview and basic mission principles. I appreciate his reading the manuscript from a missiological point of view offering important insights.

Phil Barrera is a graphic designer whose talents earn him more than I could ever afford. He asked for the privilege to design the cover for this book and then redid all of the graphics and charts within. He and his wife, Kim, have been strong supporters of our ministry and have traveled with us on several occasions to teach and encourage national leaders.

The final acknowledgements go to my team from Pleasant Word Publishing who have been the obstetricians who have helped with the final delivery. Thanks go to Tammy Hopf, my project manager who showed such godly patience to a first time author with a crazy travel schedule. I also want to thank Laura Davis who gave the text its final editing.

Without this team, these lessons would still be scribbled teaching notes scattered through a weak filing system.

INTRODUCTION

God has used three very crucial events in my life that formed the background to our ministry and the book you have in your hands. The first took place when, after fourteen years in the ministry, I survived one of the lowest points of my leadership career. I had been leading a church in Arizona for nine years and the ministry was going well. However, I experienced a period of self-doubt caused by turmoil within the church. The storm had been calmed but my doubts about my leadership continued. At this time the church had hired a financial administrator and asked that I take him to a training seminar for church administrators.

As our new team member went to his seminar on church finances, I attended sessions designed for church leaders. The teacher, a well-known corporate consultant, spent two days lecturing on how to find the right person for a job. He said, "As we discuss this concept, let's use the profile for a senior pastor in a growing church as our example." For two days, as I watched him build and explain his list of credentials, I fell deeper and deeper into my depression. I only had one of the ten qualifications on his list—a master's degree (the one qualification he saw as optional). I went home convinced that I did not belong in leadership. His list included advanced education, record of success, charismatic personality, and several dynamic leadership skills.

God led me through that time and into a study of what Scripture teaches about leadership. As I studied I began to teach others the principles I was learning. It was then that the second event took place. I was asked to teach these principles to a mission team serving in Africa. After our sessions, one of the nationals asked, "When will you return to teach my people these principles?" I truly believed that I had experienced a once-in-a-lifetime trip and that I would never be overseas again. However, the man's question shouted in my mind for the next five years.

The third event took place the year after our African trip when seven young people from our church, including our oldest son, left for college to prepare for leadership within the church. I had started my doctoral studies at Fuller with a curriculum that emphasized leadership. Concerned that I had never had any leadership training or mentoring prior to my

Introduction

entrance into the ministry, I wanted to do something to help these seven young leaders. Therefore, I chose to write my dissertation on how a leader begins in ministry. I never dreamed that this writing would result in an international ministry. A man from Poland, who had come to the states to work on his master's degree, asked me to mentor him. Then he asked me to come and teach. I was then invited to Korea, then Cambodia, then Myanmar. My wife and I started using our vacation periods to travel and teach. Seeing the need for leadership training, and the hunger of national church leaders for learning, I resigned my ministry in Anaheim, California, and we became "Traveling Teachers" with New Mission Systems International.

As we traveled we became aware of two realities. First, power-based church leadership philosophy is common in most countries. This is a product of secular philosophies, controlling expatriate models and poor translations of Scriptures. This has stifled growth and fostered sectarianism in many fertile mission fields. As we teach, people constantly tell us, "No one has taught us this before. We did not know the Bible said so much about being a leader."

Second, we became aware of how few books and resources are available for leaders in developing countries. In every country people have begged us to put our teaching into book form. This book is a result of a promise I have made to national leaders on four continents to spell out what God says in His Word about being a Kingdom Leader.

I have come to firmly believe that God's ideals for leadership are not according to the common thinking of our times. If fact, most people reading what God desires would say His principles were strange, or very uncommon. That is because, as God announced through the Prophet Isaiah, He had a higher way of thinking and acting (Isa 55:8-9). God's way will not resonate with the world's way.

Throughout Scripture we have a consistent picture of God's higher way of thinking and acting. God has not changed the way He wants things done. Therefore, if we are to be leaders in His Kingdom, we must return to His higher way and risk the world telling us that our leadership practices are uncommon.

Two days after the September 11, 2001 terrorist attacks on New York and Washington our son, Dean, now Senior Pastor of Pathways Church in Mill Creek, WA, was scheduled to preach in the convocation at Hope International University in Fullerton, California. He had to drive from Arizona because all planes were grounded. On that occasion he preached a sermon on courage. I asked him to please write that message for the last chapter of this book. I hope leaders are as blessed by it as were those attending that convocation on September 13, 2001.

I pray that this book will help you take the risk to become all God designed you to be. I write this book believing that God's principles are for men and women in every culture throughout the world. I hope you will enjoy reading it and that you will make the choice to recapture and recommit yourself to God's higher ways of thinking and acting as leaders.

CHAPTER ONE

UNCOMMON THINKING

"Whoever wants to become great among you must be your servant."
—Matthew 20:26

Jesus came to introduce the Kingdom of God in the world. He preached the message of the Kingdom. He continually used stories designed to help us understand the Kingdom. He instructed His disciples, "As you go, preach this message: 'The Kingdom of Heaven is near'" (Mt 10:7).[1] As the Church, we have been commissioned to take the message of the Kingdom to every people group on the face of the earth (Mt 28:19-20). The purpose of this study is to investigate what leadership in that Kingdom is to look like.

The study of leadership is an exciting challenge and a frightening responsibility. It is exciting because it can put leaders in touch with concepts and skills that can bring growth to the church and the confidence to face a changing world. It is frightening because of the awesome responsibility leaders face knowing that their directions and decisions make a lasting impact on the daily lives of people.

A Different Way Of Thinking About Leadership

In teaching the leadership principles of the Kingdom, one has to be extremely careful that God's Word remains the authority. The wise King Solomon warned us that "... of the writing of books, there's no end" (Ecc 12:12). This is especially true when it comes to leadership theory.

Without a clear definition and some specific instruction in Kingdom principles, a leader is tempted to look to the secular world for examples. American church leaders tend to rush off to conferences and seminars to hear the latest philosophy of the current popular leader. They purchase books and cassettes of the well-known authors. However, we have this warning,

> The approach [of studying the philosophies of the well-known leaders] has dangers. In the world around us excellence is defined by success, and success is measured by out-performing one's competitors in pursuit of money, growth and power. Christians can learn from the [others],

but we must learn with our eyes open. Our goals differ and our resources are greater.[2]

In countries where seminars and books are not so available, leaders turn to what is obtainable. One young Asian evangelist told us he got his example of leadership from watching American TV shows that were beamed into his village. Others are looking to their local military for leadership examples or to the government or to tribal traditions. Many Christian leaders copy the style of the missionary who brought them the gospel. I would like to say this imitation is a good thing, however that has not always been our experience.

If we are going to truly understand leadership in God's Kingdom, we must learn a different way of thinking. We cannot look around for the world's examples or we will not be effective in ministry. The way God expects Kingdom Leaders to act and think is different than the world's way. To draw our thinking up to His level, God speaks through the prophet Isaiah.

> "For my thoughts are not your thoughts, neither are your ways my ways," declares the LORD. "As the heavens are higher than the earth, so are my ways higher than your ways and my thoughts than your thoughts."
> —Isa 55:8-9

God wanted His people to know that Kingdom thinking is not worldly wisdom. The theories and philosophies of the world are based upon man's observations and understandings (Col 2:8).

I believe that God established His order of relationships in the Garden of Eden. Every action of God was on behalf of the two He placed there. He cared for them and fellowshipped with them. He was aware of their needs and used His power to meet those needs. The picture in the Garden of Eden is far removed from what we see of man-made gods whose relationship can only be identified as harassment.

As we travel throughout the world we encounter people groups and villages that have "personal gods." These deities must be constantly appeased in order to prevent an individual, family or village from being tormented. One scholar studying pagan deities wrote, "Not to sacrifice to the gods, to neglect their rites, to profane their shrines, or to encroach in any way upon their privileges was to invite disastrous consequences."[3]

The beauty of the Garden relationships was torn asunder by the entrance of one who had tried to usurp God's power and failed. He tried to get God's two special children to see the need to raise the level of their power, to become equals with God (Ge 3:5)—the very goal he had failed to achieve (Isa 14:14-15). The serpent reasoned with the woman and convinced her that what he was saying seemed right. When she took the fruit, chaos began to reign in mankind's relationship, and the beauty of what God established began to spiral downward.

Uncommon Thinking

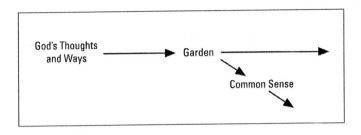

The writer of Proverbs admits that there is a way of thinking that is different than God's. He calls it a way that "seems right" (Pr 16:25). I call this *common sense*. We live in a secular world where *common sense* is based on what everyone else is doing and everyone else is doing what seems right within his or her own value system (Jdg 21:25). Even today, God's children continue to make decisions based on what seems right or through a pooling of common sense rather than on God's higher way.

The thinking God designed for His Kingdom still remains unchanged from the beginning. It is higher and purer than that which has deteriorated into common sense. Its value system is unchanged and remains the source of blessing for those who follow. Therefore, if we are to lead in the Kingdom, we must recapture a higher level of thinking than that which is considered common.

The common thinking of Jesus' time was established in the teachings of Plato and Aristotle. These two men articulated the common thinking of their era, published it and taught it as doctrine. Both men believed and taught that power was the ultimate goal of men.[4]

Greek poets and philosophers, including Plato, were students of what took place among the gods on the mythological Mount Olympus. From the Greek gods they formulated much of their thinking about man's relationship to man. However, even Plato admitted that those who studied Greek deities had "ascribed to the gods everything that is a shame and a reproach amongst men, stealing and committing adultery and deceiving each other."[5] Nevertheless, they were held up as examples of right and power, much the same as our modern world elevates politicians, sports figures, the wealthy and others we consider successful.

Plato wrote that the Aristocracy (Greek word meaning, "rule of the best")[6] or the Guardians, should govern the nation. This thinking produced constant power struggles among Greek politicians and slave owners. The Best were meant to rule; therefore it was considered good to plot the demise of another in order to show your strength. Leadership became the display of wealth, power and control.

Jesus openly attacked the Greek philosophy in Matthew 23, where He exposed the practices of Jewish leaders who were following the common thinking of the times. They commanded people to do things they were unwilling to do (23:2-4). They wore fancy clothing and demanded seats of honor (23:5-7). They gloried in their titles (23:8-12). They believed they could decide who could have a relationship with God and who could not (23:13-14). Every position that Jesus attacked in this sermon was the result of the Pharisees' failure to lead according to God's higher way.

Plato believed some men were born to power and other men were meant to be Auxiliaries (warriors). The rest of men and all women were born to be Producers and to be subservient to those above them.[7]

Alexander the Great, a student of Aristotle, believed that the philosophy of Plato was so important that he forced the nations he conquered to give up their language, heritage and culture and accept the Greek way. Even though Greece fell to Rome, Roman culture had already been thoroughly indoctrinated in Plato's philosophy and therefore continued with power-based thinking.[8]

After three hundred years of Plato's power-based philosophy, Jesus entered the picture. James and John had grown up in a Jewish culture so dominated by the concept of "power" that it had become the common way of thinking. Therefore, it was only natural when they heard Jesus speaking of a coming Kingdom that they should be the first to grab positions of importance. This was their chance to move from lowly Producers to Aristocracy.

No other place in Scripture refutes "that which seems right" more clearly than in the words of Jesus to His disciples when they argued with James and

John about who deserved positions of power in the new kingdom.

> Jesus called [his disciples] together and said, "You know that the rulers of the Gentiles lord it over them, and their high officials exercise authority over them. Not so with you. Instead, whoever wants to become great among you must be your servant, and whoever wants to be first must be your slave—just as the Son of Man did not come to be served, but to serve, and to give his life as a ransom for many."
> —Mt. 20:25-28

Jesus made it very clear that leadership in the Kingdom will not be patterned after what seems right to the world's thinking. Jesus said, "My kingdom is not of this world" (Jn 18:36). Therefore, God's Kingdom will be different than any other kingdom of this world. Leaders will be required to have a servant's heart that thinks beyond self to the greater good of those being served.

Uncommon Leadership:

A relationship of service dedicated to assisting people and/or groups to reach their potential.

Joseph: An Uncommon Leader

The Old Testament patriarch, Joseph, is an example of one who was willing to think beyond

Uncommon Thinking

self to the greater good of those being served. His example of uncommon leadership thinking has been chosen because he predates Plato's theories and demonstrates that God's model of leadership was established prior to the New Testament. In each of the three Egyptian leadership roles in which he served, he epitomized a man who trusted God's way. In each we will see the components of the definition of leadership presented in this chapter.

When the slave traders arrived in Egypt they were able to sell the handsome young man to Potiphar, the captain of the guard. As a servant in Potiphar's house Joseph dedicated himself to the honor of his owner and helped him to become prosperous in "house and field" (Ge 39:5).

Having been accused of attempting to sexually molest Potiphar's wife, Joseph was thrown in prison. God was with him and soon his servant attitude and capable skills found favor in the warden's eyes. Joseph was given responsibility for all that was done in the prison (Ge 39:22). He did his job so well that the Scripture says that the "…captain had no concerns" (Ge 39:23).

When God intervened and delivered Joseph from prison and exalted him to governor of Egypt, he took with him the same servant attitude. He dedicated himself to saving Egypt from starvation and worked to help the nation prepare for and survive a seven-year drought (Ge 41:35-36).

Sometimes, the greatest strength demonstrated by servant leaders is what they do not do. The

Scriptures refer to this as meekness, or "the restraining of power."[9] It is much easier to allow one's emotions to burst forth to display anger or control. It takes a composed person to withhold those emotions in order to meet the greater needs of those being served. Joseph demonstrated this ability very clearly when his brothers arrived in need of food. A common person could have very easily justified getting even. However, Joseph demonstrates an uncommon attitude of servanthood as he meets their needs, restores the relationship and claims the circumstances to be God's plan for good (Ge 50:20).

At no time in any of his leadership situations do we find Joseph misusing position or power. Even when they are granted as a result of his service, he continues to show a "servant-based" heart rather than "power-based" authoritarianism. With Joseph as our example, let's look at the different components of our leadership definition.

Leadership Is a Relationship

The very heart of servant leadership is found in relationship. Joseph had to have a good relationship with Potiphar to desire to bring the success to his house that was accomplished. He had a good relationship with the people in prison as they trusted him and confided in him. After Joseph's leadership success in Egypt, as Governor of the Land, (Ge 42:6) he meets his unsuspecting brothers. His desire for a relationship with them overcame the harsh feelings of their betrayal and allowed him to indeed become their leader.

God displayed the relationship in leadership when He walked in the Garden with Adam and Eve. (Ge 3:8). He was very aware of His children and their needs. He noticed when Adam was lonely and made a helper for him. (Ge 2:18). God's relationship with Adam and Eve was so opposite of the Mount Olympus relationships upon which Plato built his concepts of leadership. The Greek gods were very separated from the mortals and were bothered by their prayers.

The Incarnation of Jesus Christ is the supreme example of relationship in leading. John tells us, "The Word [Jesus] became flesh and dwelt among us" (Jn 1:14). He did not rule from afar. He did not choose twelve men and send them to school with angels as their mentors. Rather, he came and walked with those twelve for over three years. He built relationships with the rich, the poor, the elite and the outcast. It was a relationship that caused us to "love him because He first loved us" (1Jn 4.19). Jesus built a relationship to which we have responded.

Leadership author John Maxwell writes, "People do not care how much you know until they know how much you care."[10] The strongest form of leadership is "leadership by permission"—"because I see that you care, I give you permission to be my leader." That can only be granted through an uncommon relationship.

Leadership Is a Service

Somewhere between Canaan and Egypt, Joseph developed a servant attitude. The pride he demonstrated when he announced the vision of his brothers bowing to him certainly was gone. As a slave in Potiphar's house he became a model of servanthood. Even when he was falsely imprisoned he kept a servant attitude. The warden made him responsible for all that was done in the prison (Ge 39:22).

Joseph displayed no pride in his new position or power. Notice the wording used to describe his spirit. Joseph realized that two prisoners were acting depressed (Ge 40:6-7). He did not scold, whip or degrade them, as would a power-based leader expressing his authority. Rather, he showed concern for them. The Scripture says he "attended" them (Ge 40:4). The Hebrew word means he gave "menial service" or "waited upon" them.[11] He could have had them punished for not carrying their load, but he treated them with the heart of a servant. He sought their greater good. And God blessed his leadership.

The most common misconception about leadership is that it is equated with a title, position and the acquisition of power. In seminars I often put on little skits to demonstrate what leadership is not. It is not a person standing over people and telling them to go or to come. It is not sitting in judgment over whether a decision or action is right or wrong. It is not scolding people for their failure to live up to expectations. These wrong concepts of leadership are born out of wrong ideas about God. He is commonly called a "God of Wrath" rather than the scriptural revelation of Him as a "God of love" (1Jn 4:8). If we are going to raise our thinking to God's level and expectations, we must become like Him and return to a "servant-base."

The disciples reflected the common philosophy as they debated over who was the most important and worthy to hold position and title in the New Kingdom. But Jesus corrected them when he said, "…the greatest will be the servant of all."

Service is an action word. It must be seen in action in order to be properly defined. So it is with leadership. Joseph demonstrated this attitude throughout his leadership tenure. Jesus taught that if we are going to amount to anything within His Kingdom, we must give up the ideas of titles and position and look for ways to meet people's needs.

Leadership Is Dedicated Service

The word *dedicated* was chosen for this definition because it describes purpose and commitment. We could substitute the word *intentional*. Paul tells Timothy that the person who set his heart on leadership in the church desires a noble task (1Ti 3:1). This one qualification for leadership is often overlooked in churches. Little consideration is given as to whether or not the person has a heart set on taking care of the needs of people.[12] Peter emphasizes willingness twice in his instructions to Kingdom Leaders (1Pe 5:1-4).

Dedicated not only describes purpose, it also speaks of a commitment that does not give up easily. Once again Joseph demonstrated this characteristic. In each of the three venues into which he was thrust, Joseph puts heart and soul into doing his best. We do not see him sulking in his situation. We do not see him taking advantage of power. Instead we find this young man purposefully giving all he has to provide for the greater good of others.

Working with people is not an easy task. The Scriptures describe us as sheep, and sheep are not easy animals to care for. Therefore, the person who accepts leadership responsibility must be dedicated to staying and helping serve through good and bad.

Leadership Gives Assistance

Assist was chosen for this definition because it describes the ministry of the Godhead. Jesus came to serve (Mt. 20:28). The Holy Spirit has been sent to "stand beside us"[13] in order to teach us all things and will remind us of everything Jesus has said (Jn. 14:26). The responsibility of a leader should be no less than the example of the One who came to establish this Kingdom we have chosen. Leaders are teachers and helpers. "[Pharaoh] made [Joseph] master of his household, ruler over all he possessed, to instruct his princes as he pleased and teach his elders wisdom" (Ps. 105:21-22).

Joseph spent seven years instructing and assisting Egyptians to prepare for famine. Jesus spent three years instructing and assisting disciples to prepare them for ministry. Paul told the leaders at Ephesus that their purpose was to " … to prepare God's people for works of service" (Eph 4:11). The modern word for this leadership responsibility is *empowerment*. We best accomplish this when we are standing beside people, rather than "lording it over" them

Leaders Lift People to their Potential

Apparently God opened Joseph's eyes to the grain-growing potential of the Egyptian people. Regardless of how much they were producing, it is obvious that there was no storage for troubled times. Joseph worked with the people so that their harvests went far beyond their annual needs. He helped them learn how to store grain and construct structures that would keep it useable for seven years.

Many people have a rather low estimation of their own abilities. It would be much easier to give a listing of their personal weaknesses rather than their strengths. Just as Joseph challenged the people of Egypt to grow the amount of grain he knew they were capable of producing, leaders look for the potential in people and assist them in reaching it.

When Jesus met Simon, he told him that his new name would be Peter—The Rock. At first, we do not see any of the strength that Jesus saw in Peter. But Jesus stayed with him, taught him, corrected him, forgave him and commissioned him. As a result, we can look back on this great man of God and say that

Peter truly became 'the rock' Jesus saw in him. Jesus assisted him to reach his potential.

The concept of dedicating oneself to assisting others to reach their potential is found throughout the biblical narrative. Nehemiah speaks of accomplishing "what God put on his heart to do for Jerusalem" (Ne 2:12). He did this by standing beside his people, working with them and encouraging them in what he knew they could accomplish. Paul was constantly seeking the best for those on his team and in the churches he served. Fourteen times in his letters Paul uses the concept of building people.

Robert Greenleaf, in his classic study on Servant Leadership, sums up the task with this evaluative question on effective leadership:

> "A servant-leader is a servant first...[A leader's responsibility is] to make sure other people's highest priority needs are being served. The best test, and difficult to administer, is do those served grow as persons? Do they, while being served, become healthier, wiser, freer, more autonomous, more likely themselves to become servants?"[14]

Conclusion

Joseph, a man chosen by God long before Plato penned his famous dialogues, demonstrates the type of leadership God expects for his people. It is leadership that sees the needs of people and comes alongside them to help them meet those needs.

Uncommon Thinking

Alexander the Great forced Plato's concepts of power on the civilized world. Three hundred years later Jesus stepped into a world where this power-based philosophy was accepted—it had become common. Jesus taught His followers a different type of leadership to be practiced in His Kingdom, a philosophy of service. However, with power accepted as common, it did not take long for the church to revert back to its allure.

> People are more comfortable seeing a representative of God than being directly in communion with the Living One…thus they began to set up structures and leadership not unlike the well-known Jewish and pagan infrastructures. They soon forgot that Jesus was the head of the body as they began to transfer His leadership to human leaders and the supporting administrative structures.[15]

Therefore, the church began patterning itself after the Roman power-based system of titles and positions. As the church trained and sent out missionaries, they took the power-based philosophy with them and taught people in new worlds to interpret Scripture based on Plato's worldview rather than a biblical worldview.

Until the Church is willing to return to God's uncommon ways, it will continue to clash over titles, positions and questions of authority. While it continues to copy common ideas from the secular worldview it will remain enmeshed in board meetings, committee reports, rules of order and power struggles. In the meantime God's people are not assisted in reaching their potential for doing the work God designed for His Kingdom.

CHAPTER TWO

UNCOMMON MEASUREMENTS

> We do not dare to classify or compare ourselves with some who commend themselves. When they measure themselves by themselves and compare themselves with themselves, they are not wise.
> —2 Corinthians 10:12

I had the privilege of beginning my ministry experience in Thousand Oaks, California, a new, fast-growing city west of Los Angeles. The rolling hills and ocean breezes lured thousands of people out of the congestion and smog of the big city. When I arrived to be the youth pastor of a newly planted church, I was amazed at the number of new homes being constructed. However, as I arrived people were just beginning to learn a new meaning to "paradise lost."

An unscrupulous builder had detected that there were no firm building codes or inspections in this new area. Therefore, he cut corners on every principle of house building. It was not uncommon to sit in a home and to see sunlight shining through ceilings and walls. These wide gaps had appeared as a result of crumbling foundations. When building engineers were called in, inspections revealed that the homes had been built on thin foundations with no reinforcing steel. Soon, beautiful homes began to fall apart as the ground under them shifted and settled.

The same problem presents itself in building leadership for the Kingdom of God. We must make a decision about the type of foundation upon which we build the church and its leadership and what building blocks we use to build upon that foundation. There is a strong temptation to look at the world and copy the leadership principles presented by famous authors. However, if our leadership is based on the wrong foundation, it well fall apart. Perhaps this is partly what Jesus had in mind when he told the Parable of the Wise and Foolish Builders. The one who hears and obeys will stand (Mt 7:24-27).

I have sat in the homes and offices of church leaders all around the world. It is not unusual to hear stories of how their leadership began to crack and, for some, to crumble around them. The world's philosophy of leadership looked good, but when they put it into practice it could not withstand the tests. I found myself talking to leaders ready to quit. Their passion for ministry had disintegrated and they did not know if they wanted to continue. Or, if they lived in a culture that does not accept quitting, they continue with no heart and no vision of what can happen. They had built on a faulty foundation.

CHOOSING OUR MEASURING POINT

The Apostle Paul teaches us that the church is built upon the "foundation of the apostles and prophets" (Eph 2:20), which is God's revealed word. Every word of that revelation is "God breathed" and is profitable for our use in any life situation, including leadership (2Ti 3:16-17). Peter reminds us that no Scripture is result of the author's imagination (2Pe 1:19-21). If we are to build God's Kingdom in God's way, then the Scriptures become God's foundation for our message and leadership.

In biblical times, the first stone laid upon the foundation was the cornerstone. It was a perfect stone from which every measurement in the building would be computed. To understand the cornerstone for God's Kingdom, Old and New Testament authors pointed to The Messiah as "The Cornerstone" (Is. 28:16; Zec 10:4; Eph 2:20). We are told that all the prophecies of Scripture point to Jesus (Rv 19:10). His ministry and sacrifice were the message of the apostles (1Co 15:3). He is The Cornerstone from which all measurements in the building process are to be made.

Solid leadership must be built on a solid foundation and have a perfect cornerstone from which to make all its measurements. Jesus is that Cornerstone (Eph 2:20). Everything in Scripture and the church must be measured from Jesus—that is the purpose of a cornerstone.

God's principles for leadership are not hidden. The teachings and examples of godly leadership that are clearly portrayed in Scripture are very different from what is held in common. The Bible clearly warns Kingdom Leaders not to copy the behaviors and customs of this world (Ro 12:2). If we truly believe the Bible is given as a blueprint from God and Jesus is its cornerstone, we will measure our motives and actions from Him and our uncommon leadership will become uncommonly strong.

The world will see the biblical measurements for leadership as uncommon; however, I am convinced that God will honor those who return to his higher thinking.

Choosing Our Building Blocks

The building blocks of Kingdom Leadership are the qualities the Scripture uses to measure a leader. The world has a totally different list of qualifications for leadership than that which we discover in God's Word. Even when the church and the world use the same words, we find that when the definitions are measured from the Cornerstone, they are different.

Uncommon Measurements

It will be discovered that biblical definitions for leadership building blocks are uncommon.

As we turn our attention to some of the six building blocks for Kingdom Leadership we will discuss them in their order of importance for building a strong church.

Building Blocks of Leadership

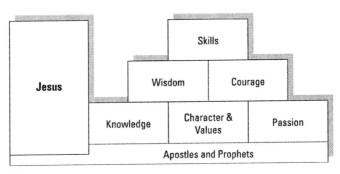

Building Blocks of Leadership – Character and Values

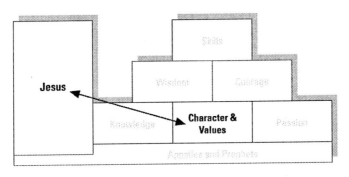

Character and Values

This middle block is the key to the all six. Jesus and those who penned the Scriptures taught more on character than on any other leadership subject. Character formation was the foundation to Jesus' Sermon on the Mount. In this important session recorded by Matthew, Jesus taught on godly attitudes (5:1-12), reconciliation (5:21-26), faithfulness (5:27-32), integrity (5:33-37), forgiveness (5:38-42), humility (6:1-4), priorities (6:19-24) and other character values. He sums it all up in the ability to love God and others (5:43-48; 22:37-40).

Character is the fruit of God's Spirit dwelling within us (Gal 5:22-23). The qualifications or measurements of a leader in the New Testament church deal almost entirely with character. If we would remove this building block the wall would collapse.

We can trace the swing of common thinking from an emphasis on *character ethic* to an emphasis on *personality ethic*. "Success became more a function of personality, of public image, of attitudes and behaviors, skills and techniques, that lubricate the processes of human interaction."[1]

The emphasis on personality over character is partly to blame for some of the political and corporate meltdowns experienced in the world and, unfortunately, the church. Leaders have been more concerned about their own personal desires rather than those of their people. We have had a recurrence of what was taking place in the days of Ezekiel when the people God depended upon for leadership were more concerned with taking care of themselves than seeing to the needs of the people entrusted to their care (Eze 34:2).

It is not hard to trace the background for such selfish reasoning. Our study can go from Ezekiel to Plato to Machiavelli, a famous leadership author of the sixteenth century. His book, *The Prince,* is still considered by many today as an important study for leaders. In it he plainly teaches that integrity and character consistency are not always good for a leader.

> I shall be so bold as to assert this: that having [good character qualities] and practicing them at all times is harmful: and appearing to have them is useful; for instance, to seem merciful, faithful, humane, forthright, religious, and to be so; but [the leader's] mind should be disposed in such a way that should it become necessary not to be so, he will be able and know how to change to the contrary. And it is essential to understand this: that a [leader], and especially a new [leader], cannot observe all those things by which men are considered good.[2]

When leaders are more concerned about achieving and maintaining their position of power than their integrity, it creates a "we-they" mindset. Leaders separate themselves from others to show that they are more qualified to control their followers. What other people are experiencing only concerns the leader if it threatens his position or gives a possibility for strengthening his position of leadership. There is no sense of caring or working for each other.

There is a drastic contrast between the leadership profiles created by secular leaders and the measurements penned by the Apostle Paul. The common thinking is to put an emphasis on personality, looks, experience, oral skills and abilities to keep people aligned with a vision. With the exception of "apt to teach," Paul's entire list has some very uncommon qualifications, all dealing with a person's character.

> The overseer must be above reproach, the husband of but one wife, temperate, self-controlled, respectable, hospitable, able to teach, not given to drunkenness, not violent but gentle, not quarrelsome, not a lover of money. He must manage his own family well...He must not be a recent convert...He must also have a good reputation with outsiders...
> Deacons, likewise, are to be men worthy of respect, sincere, not indulging in much wine, and not pursuing dishonest gain. They must keep hold of the deep truths of the faith with a clear conscience...
> In the same way, their wives [deaconesses] are to be women worthy of respect, not malicious talkers but temperate and trustworthy in everything.
> —1Ti 3:1-11

I had a seminary professor who defined leadership as "character molded by a love relationship for the Lord and his people."³ A leader fulfilling this definition will always make decision based on what is best for those being led. Because of their relationship to their people, they will constantly keep a vigilant watch on needs and a constant eye on the future and what opportunities and/or threats lie therein.

Building Blocks of Leadership - Knowledge

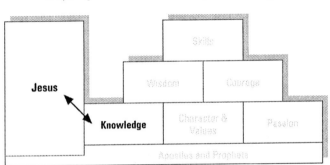

Knowledge

Common thinking would choose a leader based on knowledge, education and experience. God, however, chooses people for their willingness to learn. God chose people for leadership who had no specific knowledge for what He was asking. Nevertheless, once they accepted God's call, the gaining of that knowledge became of prime importance to them. David was not raised in the courts of leadership. He was a shepherd and spent much of the first part of his life hiding from leaders. Yet, he craved knowledge—even that which he discovered through the study of God's creation,

> Day after day [the heavens] pour forth speech;
> night after night they display knowledge. There
> is no speech or language where their voice is not
> heard. Their voice goes out into all the earth,
> their words to the ends of the world.
> —Ps 19:2-4

As we read through the Psalms we discover that David never felt he knew all he needed to know to fully follow God and to be the leader of his people. He constantly desired that God would teach him "His path" (way) (Ps 25:4-5; 27:11; 143:8). He prayed for an understanding of God's decrees (Ps 119:12). He inquired of God to teach him His will (Ps 143:10). Moses prayed, "If you are pleased with me, teach me your ways so I may know you and continue to find favor with you. Remember that this nation is your people" (Ex 33:13).

Jonah had been a pastor in Thailand over thirty years. As a young man he planted churches in China until he was forced to leave behind his wife and two sons and escape into Burma. Shortly after his escape his wife died of Malaria and he was never again to see his sons. For twenty years he planted churches in his new country until once again he was forced to flee under threat of persecution. He arrived in Thailand and continued serving God's people. Three years in a row Jonah attended our leadership seminars, sitting in the front row taking notes like these were the only classes he would ever take. In his eighty-fifth year I asked him, "Jonah, why do you still attend these seminars?" He answered, "Because, I still have so much to learn."

The writer of Proverbs says that it is not good to have "zeal without knowledge" (19:2). Therefore, competent leaders will always be learning and adding to their ability to lead and to grow other leaders. They are students of God's Word. They seek out training that will help them better serve their people. They listen and learn from accomplished leaders as well as those who are being led. A church or organization with a leader who already "knows it all" will stop growing as their leader becomes stagnant.

The Scriptures never describe God calling a person to leadership based on the knowledge that individual possesses. However, all the effective leaders God called were successful because they were willing to learn everything God had for them.

Building Blocks of Leadership - Passion

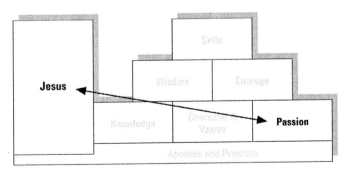

Passion

According to the Oxford English Dictionary, the word *passion* describes "an intense enthusiasm."[4] From the Latin word *to suffer* (Oxford Dictionary) *passion* pictures a person who feels he must accept his heart's calling. Not to do so would be *to suffer*.

Common leadership philosophy speaks much about passion. However, the common ideal is to find a person who has a passion to succeed at any cost. One hears of a person who is "devoted to the company," a person willing to suffer for the company over and above family and faith. Kate Wendleton, an American who helps out-of-work leaders find new jobs, describes the common measurement of passion.

> "Now the employer has the power. And guess what? They say, 'I'm going to work you to the bone, and just be glad you have a job, and if you get a divorce it's a sign of your devotion [passion] to the company.'"[5]

And yet, the uncommon measurement of Kingdom Leadership contemplates a person's passion to serve. They would suffer if the sufferings of others were not lessened.

Nehemiah was guided by that which "God had put on his heart to do" (2:12). He is recognized as one of the greatest of all the biblical leaders because of his desire for God and for God's people. Paul writes of being "compelled to preach the gospel"

(1Co 9:16). Although passion is not always present at the beginning of a leadership call (it was absent in Moses at the burning bush) it becomes the fire that burns within the leader's heart to take God's people to where God wants them to be. Jeremiah describes it:

> But if I say, "I will not mention him or speak any more in his name," His word is in my heart like a fire, a fire shut up in my bones. I am weary of holding it in; indeed, I cannot".
> —20:9

Both Paul and Jeremiah indicate that they would *suffer* if they did not live out what they believed they were called to do.

When my sons were involved with Boy Scouts of America, I became a scout leader. I wanted to spend time with my sons, and it also provided an opportunity to share my faith with and teach future leaders. As a new scout leader I was required to attend a training session. One night while we were gathered around a fire we were asked to share why we desired to be scout leaders. Over half of the men in our circle shared that they really didn't know why they were there. The bishop in their church told them that they had to come. There was no enthusiasm for their assignment. As I continued in monthly leadership meetings I noticed frequent absenteeism and a great turnover among those leaders who had no passion for their responsibility.

I could make a long list of the poor reasons I have been given for why certain people were made leaders in the church. For example, church members were continuing in sin, but the church hoped that appointing them to leadership would straighten them out. In other instances members were inactive or sporadic in church attendance, but someone thought that making them a leader would inspire them to attend more often. The list could include those who were chosen because of status, business ownership or giving ability. There were also good members who possessed no desire to lead, yet were begged until they finally consented.

Paul describes a potential church leader as one who "sets his heart" on that ministry (1Ti 3:1). Without a heart for ministry there will be absenteeism, resistance to training, and potential power problems caused by a misunderstanding of purpose and direction. A leader must be a person who has a heart to fulfill the mandate God has given His Church.

Building Blocks of Leadership - Wisdom

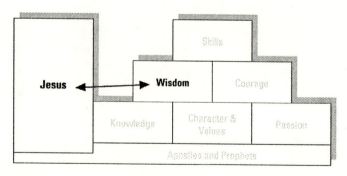

Uncommon Measurements

Wisdom

God was pleased with Solomon because of his answer when he had the opportunity to ask for anything from God's hand. Instead of seeking power and wealth, he requested the wisdom and knowledge to lead God's people (1Ch 1:10). God responded to Solomon's unselfishness and desire for godly leadership by giving him both wisdom and riches. God's response to Solomon gives evidence to how He will measure current Kingdom Leaders.

Therefore, the first stone in the second row of Leadership Building blocks is wisdom. Simply put, wisdom melds knowledge, passion and skills. Most observers have seen people who have gained much learning through study or life experience, but have shown an inability to apply that knowledge. There are people who have a dynamic personality but don't have the wisdom to control it. Wisdom pulls all the contents of our life together and understands where and how to use them.

Solomon, in his godly wisdom, describes for us this important building block in our leadership profile. We learn that wisdom provides discipline, prudence and a sense of justice (Pr 1:3). The leader who attains wisdom will have knowledge, discretion and guidance (Pr 1:4-5). Attaining this quality is more advantageous to a leader than acquiring gold, silver or rubies (Pr 3:14-15). Solomon writes, "blessed is the man who finds wisdom" (Pr 3:13).

According to King Solomon and the Apostle James, wisdom is available to those who would ask for it (Pr 2:6; Jas 1:5-6). Leaders need to seek after it more than they would seek for position and title. To make sure our thinking is clear on what God offers the Kingdom Leader, James contrasts godly wisdom with the power-based wisdom of Greek philosophy. To be "wise in the ways of the world" one must show ambition, be self-promoting, and assert the power necessary to overcome others (causing envy and bitterness) (3:14-15). James says that the wisdom from God that is offered to Kingdom Leaders brings humility (3:13); it is "peace-loving, considerate, submissive, full of mercy and good fruit, impartial and sincere" (3:17).

The writer of Chronicles halts his genealogical listing of the Israelite tribes to mention the "men of Issachar who understood the times and knew what to do" (1Ch 12:32). These men knew the reality of Israel's current condition. They understood what was happening in their country and culture and had the wisdom to know what needed to be done to strengthen the nation. It is this ability to see and understand, coupled with the character described by James, which will bring positive growth to God's Kingdom.

Building Blocks of Leadership - Courage

Jesus ⟷ Courage

(Building blocks shown faintly: Skills, Wisdom, Knowledge, Character & Values, Passion, Apostles and Prophets)

Courage

To be a person of good character is of utmost importance to Kingdom Leadership. It is extremely beneficial to combine that element of character with the passion one has for a task in the Kingdom. However, if the leader does not have the courage to see it through, Kingdom people will wander, waiting for someone to step to the front to lead. There are many good Christians who do nothing for the Kingdom. There are people who have very strong beliefs burning inside them—they can constantly talk about what they want to do. But, it takes courage to step in front of people and say, "I believe we should go this way" and start walking.

Let me suggest one possible description of courage.

> To lead is to act. To have courage is to take charge, first of one's own life, for the true hero is not the person who conquers others but the one who conquers himself or herself. Then you are ready to take charge of the organizations…courage means to act with *sustained initiative*.[6]

Koestenbaum's view of courage provides a contrast between Athens (Plato/Greek Thinking) and Jerusalem (Moses/Hebrew Thinking), "the two sources of Western thought."

> Athens defined truth as a universal theory. Truth for Athens lies in a scientific proposition. But truth for Jerusalem, exemplified perhaps most dramatically by the life and death of Jesus… lies in risking, to the death, a personal decision about what this world is, what right and wrong are, and how a human being is to live—we are given only one chance.[7]

Common thinkers believe that truth is relevant to them; they have reasoned it out in their mind and are convinced that it seems right for them. They believe that truth is different for every person. Whatever I conclude through my observations and deductions is true for me; others will have to determine what is true for them.

Uncommon thinkers believe truth is a revealed constant that they are willing to die for. Truth is *revealed* rather than *reasoned*. It takes much more courage to stand for an absolute than to change with the common winds.

Of the four main ingredients in Koestenbaum's leadership formula, he has determined that courage is the quality most frequently missing.[8] Leadership is a risk. Criticism, second-guessing and resistance are guaranteed to anyone who would step to the front. Most who would like to think of themselves as leaders are not willing to take the risk. They lack the courage to press ahead, confident that they are leading people in the direction God has revealed.

Building Blocks of Leadership - Skills

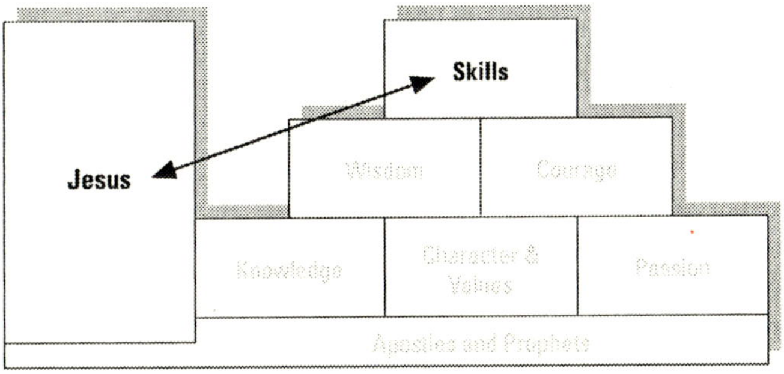

[Diagram: Pyramid of building blocks with "Jesus" on the left pointing via arrow to "Skills" at top. Middle row: Wisdom, Courage. Next row: Knowledge, Character & Values, Passion. Bottom: Apostles and Prophets]

Skills

From a biblical standpoint the top leadership building block is the one most misunderstood. There are no Scriptures attached to it, because there is no scriptural mention of leadership skills or their requirement for Kingdom Leadership. Biblical leaders demonstrate various skills. However, God never called a person based on skills. In all of the measurements of a biblical leader there is only one possible mention of a skill—an overseer must be "able to teach" (1Ti 3:2). Nevertheless, many people shy away from accepting leadership responsibility because they feel deficient in their skills.

Skills are important; that is why they are included among our building blocks. However, the common thinking of our times is to look first for skills. It is not unusual for a banker, business owner, or other well-known person to be invited to church leadership based on the fact that their position shows that they have skills. There is little thought given to a higher thinking—to character, knowledge or passion as the measurements that we should use to choose Kingdom Leaders.

Conclusion

Here we have the building blocks for Kingdom Leadership—six very important ingredients to the leadership picture. All are measured from the Cornerstone. All are important. Character, however, is purposely located in the lower center of the wall because if this one ingredient is missing, the wall is subject to collapse.

Recently I read the story of an American football player who had the skills, the knowledge and the passion to be a great professional athlete. However, the history of his character was also well known—he was trouble wherever he went. The common thinking of coaches was, "we care little about the reputation of his character; we need his talent." He was drafted to play professional football but continually broke rules and brought embarrassment to his teammates. The team cut him and another team signed him. The same problems continued. The second team let him go and a third team offered him a contract. The problems continued.

Tragically, this story is repeated in companies and churches every day. Businesses and churches are embarrassed or brought down because they choose leadership based on the common measurements for a leader (experience, skills, presence and the ability to communicate) rather than God's higher guidelines.

CHAPTER THREE

UNCOMMON PURPOSE

"The Lord does not look at the things man looks at…the Lord looks at the heart."

—1 Samuel 16:7

"The lamp of the LORD searches the spirit of a man; it searches out his inmost being."

—Proverbs 20:27

When many people hear "leadership" they begin to think of position, power and authority. King Saul had all three, plus he was tall and handsome (1 Sa 9:2). Yet, he did not find favor with God. A small shepherd boy, the youngest of seven brothers, replaced Saul. David grew to become the greatest leader in the pre-messianic history of Israel.

What made the difference? Perhaps the answer is found in the words of the Prophet Samuel when he came to tell Saul that He was being stripped of his Kingdom Leadership.

> But now your kingdom will not endure; the LORD has sought out a man after his own heart and appointed him leader of his people, because you have not kept the LORD'S command."
> —1 Sa 13:14

As Samuel went to anoint young David as the future leader of the kingdom, God gave a special qualifier to help the prophet understand whom He would choose.

> But the LORD said to Samuel, "Do not consider his appearance or his height, for I have rejected him. The LORD does not look at the things man looks at. Man looks at the outward appearance, but the LORD looks at the heart."
> —1 Sa 16:7

Three hundred years later, God was once again upset with Israel. This was not the kingdom He had hoped to have. The Israelites were still coming to the temple to offer their sacrifices. They were saying the prescribed prayers and singing the proper songs (Isa 1:10-15). What was the problem? Isaiah defines it as the same problem God saw in Saul. "These people come near to me with their mouth and honor me with their lips, but their hearts are far from me" (Isa 29:13).

Jeremiah confirmed this problem as he described the wickedness he saw in Israel (Jer 12:2). Jesus restated the prophets' indictment in Mark 7:6 when Israel's spiritual leaders accused His disciples of not keeping the oral traditions Jewish scholars had attached to the Law.

Some would say that the first ingredient for which God is searching is obedience. However, King Saul and the people during the times of Isaiah and Jeremiah would have confidently claimed obedience. The Pharisees would have vehemently denied any suggestion that they were not obedient. They were all participating in religious rituals.

To be near the heart of God or to have a heart for God means that behind every action and decision lies a desire to fulfill God's unchanging purpose (Ps 33:11; Heb 6:17). God's purpose is not fulfilled in ritualistic observances. As important as character is, God's purpose goes beyond merely living a "good moral life." People of good character can have the wrong purpose. Purpose aligns our heart and our head with our hands in action. The purpose of Kingdom Leadership is to model and perpetuate the "heart of God." To understand what that means, let us look at two views of God's heart and apply them to Kingdom Purpose.

The Nature of God's Heart

Let us go back to the Garden of Eden and ask about the purpose God had in creating it. Did He create the garden for man, or did He create man for the garden? If God's purpose was to create a beautiful garden for His pleasure, then He created man as a slave to care for it. When man failed he was dismissed from the garden to be on his own. If God constructed the garden for man, then His purpose in planting it was to provide the best for His special creation. The garden was an act of love. When man failed, God initiated a new plan to fulfill His purpose.

From the tender creation of man in the Garden of Eden to the grace shown to His creation following the death of His Son, God's heart can only be described as "love." John clearly declares, "God is love" (1Jn 4:8). In his gospel he wrote, "For God so loved the world" (Jn 3:16). Everywhere we look in the Scripture we see God's actions motivated by love. The Law given to Israel was designed to provide a quality of life beyond anything experienced in the surrounding nations. It is shown in the love of a shepherd for his sheep (Ps 23; Eze 34). It is shown in Jesus' picture of a father standing in front of his house looking and hoping for his prodigal son to return (Lk 15:11-24). The love we see described in these teachings and narratives can only be characterized as an uncommon love that streams from God's higher way of thinking and acting.

Uncommon Purpose

If we want to understand the heart of God, we need only study the ministry of Jesus. See His compassion for the hurting. Watch Him bless the children. Observe His passion for His Father's purpose for His people. Listen to Him as He offers living water to a spiritually thirsty woman at Jacob's Well (Jn 4). Notice His desire to offer "abundant life" to all that will accept it (Jn 10:10). Feel His tears as He weeps before the grave of His friend Lazarus (Jn 11). Watch Him stoop to wash His disciples' feet (Jn 13). However the greatest act of love was when He restrained His power to allow the crucifixion to continue because He knew it had to happen for our benefit.

As *love* is the descriptive word describing the nature of God's heart, it must also be the key word to describe the heart of a leader in His Kingdom. "By this all men will know that you are my disciples, if you love one another" (Jn 13:35). Love is a difficult priority for a leader who is focused on position, power and authority. Love is not a practice of a leader who is striving for his own success. Love is not the choice made by a leader who feels the need to control people and direct their lives.

As the Apostle John writes his description of Jesus' arrival on earth, three times he uses the word "grace" (Jn 1:14-17). In this paragraph John makes a very interesting statement that shows us the heart and purpose of Jesus (God in the flesh). He writes, "The law came through Moses, but grace came through Jesus Christ" (Jn 1:16). Think of grace as *love that goes beyond common sense*. Grace is love that is put into action. It is going beyond the common responses to people's problems to an uncommon response that focuses on needs. Our common response to sin and weakness is law. However, God's response, through Jesus, is grace.

> You are not under law, but under grace.
> —Ro 6:14

> I do not set aside the grace of God, for if righteousness could be gained through the law, Christ died for nothing!
> —Gal 2:21

> For if the inheritance depends on the law, then it no longer depends on a promise; but God in his grace gave it to Abraham through a promise.
> —Gal 3:18

> [We] are justified freely by his grace through the redemption that came by Christ Jesus.
> —Ro 3:24

The heart of God is an uncommon love that is demonstrated through acts of grace—forgiveness, visiting the sick, visiting prisoners, clothing the naked, feeding the hungry, etc. (Mt 25:34-46). For this reason a Kingdom Leader must base leadership in the love of God that continually deals with people on the basis of grace rather than condemnation. However, the common way of the world is to write rules and policies, create chains-of-command and dictate responsibilities. Common thinking says,

"Step up and take control." According to pastor and leadership author Henri Nouwen, it is much easier to exercise power than it is to exercise love. It is easier to control people than it is to love them.[1] It takes more leadership power and self-control to love and trust than to be autocratic.

All around the world we find leadership that has been seduced by power. Leaders establish their kingdoms rather than spreading God's Kingdom. To do this they put the emphasis on law rather than grace. Strict rules are given that cause anguish and separation, rather than grace which leads to healing and unity. Sermons are aimed at scolding people and letting them know they don't measure up, rather than the message of grace that frees and builds people.

Listen to the words of the famous Russian scholar, Alexander Solzhenitsyn,

> A society based on the letter of the law, and never reaching any higher, fails to take advantage of the full range of human possibility. The letter of the law is too cold and formal to have a beneficial influence on society. Whenever the tissue of life is woven of legalistic relationships, this creates an atmosphere of spiritual mediocrity that paralyzes men's noblest impulses."[2]

The Law defined who was accepted and who was rejected. Grace reaches out in acceptance. The Law defines sin. Grace demonstrates forgiveness. The Law binds people to rules and regulations. Grace builds people according to God's design. The Law limits people. Grace frees people. The Law exists to lead us to Jesus. Jesus came to lead us to a relationship with the Father. A Kingdom Leader must always fight the temptation of becoming more dedicated to Law than to grace, to building one's own kingdom rather than God's.

Jesus commissioned his disciples to go into the entire world and preach a message of "repentance and forgiveness of sin"(Lk 24:47). His message is good news (Lk 4:43) that emphasizes grace. Luke, the church historian, reported that Paul and Barnabas preached a "message of grace" (Ac 14:3). Wherever they taught, their emphasis was grace. It was the good news, the uncommon love that sent God to a cross so that man might be free. The leader who strives to be a person "after God's heart" must demonstrate this higher concept of love that flows from God's heart—a love that cares for and frees God's people. Even though John Killinger is writing to preachers, I believe he speaks to all Kingdom Leaders who desire God's heart.

> The preacher's first calling, therefore, is to love …We must love the community and love the people who belong to the community. It is not enough, if one wishes to preach, to be in love with preaching. It is not enough to be in love with the Christian philosophy. It is not even enough to be in love with God. We must love people and love God's vision of the community. Then we can preach.[3]

Then we can serve in the church or the community. These words are not only for those who preach, but for all who would seek to represent God in the home, community or work environment.

The Desire of God's Heart

The writer of Proverbs declared that God has a purpose that prevails above man's desires (19:21). Paul told the Ephesians that God has an "eternal purpose" that He accomplished in Jesus (3:11). The writer of Hebrews refers to God's "unchanging purpose" (6:17). If it is true that God has an unchanging purpose, then it is possible to trace it from Genesis to Revelation and test its consistency. If such a purpose can be discovered in God's heart, then a Kingdom Leader who strives for the heart of God will adopt the same purpose. Jesus said that He came to do the work of His Father (Jn 14:10); should not our goal be the same?

God's words to Israel just prior to their entrance into the Holy Land speak volumes to us concerning His desire to have a people to bless. He had chosen Israel from all the nations of the world to show His love and eagerness to bless people throughout the world. God wanted His *treasured possession* (four times Moses uses this phrase to describe Israel) to be recipients of all His blessings.

> The LORD has declared this day that you are His people, His treasured possession as He promised, and that you are to keep all His commands. He

has declared that He will set you in praise, fame and honor high above all the nations He has made and that you will be a people holy to the LORD your God, as He promised.
—Dt 26:18-19

Four hundred years earlier God had outlined his strategy to Abraham as He established His covenant with him.

The LORD had said to Abram, "Leave your country, your people and your father's household and go to the land I will show you. "I will make you into a great nation and I will bless you; I will make your name great, and you will be a blessing. I will bless those who bless you, and whoever curses you I will curse; and all peoples on earth will be blessed through you."
—Ge 12:1-3

Through the Prophet Samuel, God repeated His desire to have a people to bless. "Who is like your people Israel—the one nation on earth that God went out to redeem as a people for himself ...?" (2Sa 7:23).

God's purpose held strong for centuries, bound by the uncommon love that is His nature. This love repeatedly forgave, delivered and received back a people who had strayed from His covenant.

Israel continually rejected God's offer of blessing. Therefore, after several appeals and disciplinary actions, God chose a new people. He is calling people out of the world to be His treasured possession—people from every nation, tribe and tongue. Notice the consistency of the New Testament writers on the subject of God choosing a special people.

> God at first showed His concern by taking from the Gentiles a people for Himself.
> —Ac 15:14

> [Jesus] gave Himself for us to redeem us from all wickedness and to purify for Himself a people that are His very own, eager to do what is good.
> —Tit 2:13

> You are a chosen people, a royal priesthood, a holy nation, a people belonging to God, that you may declare the praises of him who called you out of darkness into his wonderful light. Once you were not a people, but now you are the people of God; once you had not received mercy, but now you have received mercy.
> —1Pe 2:9-10

The thread of consistency that traces God's unchanging purpose culminates in Heaven. In Revelation 21:3 the loud voice from the throne pronounces, "Now!" In this single word all of God's plans come to completion. This is what He has been hoping for, planning for and working toward since He placed Adam and Eve in the Garden of Eden. The Apostle John describes the scene:

They sang a new song: "You are worthy to take the scroll and to open its seals, because you were slain, and with your blood you purchased men for God from every tribe and language and people and nation. You have made them to be a kingdom and priests to serve our God, and they will reign on the earth."

—Rev 5:9-10

In Revelation 21:3, John describes the celebration: "I heard a loud voice from the throne saying, 'Now the dwelling of God is with men, and he will live with them. They will be his people, and God himself will be with them and be their God.'"

The Apostle John summarizes the impact of Jesus' uncommon ministry, "From the fullness of His grace we have all received one blessing after another" (Jn 1:16). Having a people of His own to bless seems to be a key to understanding God's purpose. This is the desire of His heart.

There is consistency to God's purpose from beginning to end. God's uncommon love has set a plan to call to Himself a people of His very own to bless. If this is true, then the heart of the Kingdom Leader will reflect His higher ways. A Kingdom Leader will have a passion to spread the message to the nations so that God will have a people from every corner of the world. The Kingdom Leader will bless people and treat them as God's treasure. We find no emphasis on power, no striving for position or authority that gives rule over one another. God's purpose is to bless, to build and to give abundant life. When we answer God's call to be a Kingdom Leader, our purpose must join to His.

Conclusion

A heart for God was the missing ingredient in King Saul and those "trampling" in God's courtyards during Isaiah and Jeremiah's time. Kingdom Leadership must begin where God begins. It is not a matter of self-striving. God is not searching for good-looking people with high intelligence and charismatic personalities.

What does a Kingdom Leader look like? David was a Kingdom Leader. He was recognized as a man after God's heart (Ac 13:32). He gained that distinction because "he had served God's purpose in his own generation" (Ac 13:36). David led his people with "integrity of heart" (Ps 78:72), a heart that was loyal to God (1Ki 11:4). David's life was not perfect; he made some major mistakes, but his heart still yearned to follow after God. Israel thrived under David's leadership. They walked closer to God than at any other time in their history. They became the strongest nation on the face of the earth. Because of David, Israel knew what it meant to be "the people of God's purpose."

Today a Kingdom Leader continues to be a person who has a heart of love for God and His people, demonstrating much more grace than law, and sharing God's desire to bless rather than control people. A Kingdom Leader works faithfully in ways to ensure that people grow stronger in their personal relationship to God and become more capable of taking their place in the Kingdom. The people under Kingdom Leadership know what it means to be "God's treasured possession."

CHAPTER FOUR

UNCOMMON PARADIGM

"I will place over them one shepherd, my servant David, and he will tend them; he will tend them and be their shepherd."

—Ezekiel 34:23

I was a young shepherd, but a shepherd nonetheless. Little did I know that when my brother and I started building a relationship with the Basque shepherds who brought their sheep to graze the fields near our farm that I would be learning important lessons for future leadership.

The Basque shepherds had flocks of over two hundred sheep that they would bring to graze the alfalfa fields after the year's final cutting. My brother and I met two of the shepherds; with the help of simple English and sign language we learned about sheep. One day the shepherd offered us a lamb that had been abandoned by its mother. We took it and bottle fed it. The next year we were given two more. Our father bought a ram and we began breeding our small flock. Soon we had twenty-two sheep in our tiny flock. We fed them, sheared them, searched for them when they got out, cared for them when they were sick and helped them deliver their lambs.

At the time we were learning about sheep Jesus became the shepherd to our family. We knew more about sheep than we did about Christianity. We started learning the Scriptures. When we studied John 10:1-18 about the Good Shepherd we were surprised because we already knew that about shepherds. We had seen our Basque friends tend their sheep. We knew they slept in the gate of the nightpen (Jn 10:3,7). We had seen them call their sheep by name and have those sheep respond (Jn 10:3). We knew that a shepherd always walked in front of his sheep and they followed (Jn 10:4).

In a time when the common thinking about leadership was position, power and control, Jesus came with a different paradigm—a higher way of thinking and acting. Imagine, in light of the Greek power philosophy of that day, what people might have thought when their revered leader announced himself as a Good Shepherd (Jn 10:11)? The study of Greek history is filled with wars, political coups and attempted world conquest. A study of Greek deities is a study of feuding and deceitfulness. Its narratives are annals of sons against fathers, brother against brother and Titans against Olympians. It is survival of the strongest in a quest for control. Plato looked at this and said it was good. Jesus looked at people and said they needed God's peace and care.

Although Hebrew history has its war stories, never do we find God honoring Hebrew attempts to conquer other than the land He had given them. Whereas the heroes of Greek history are conquerors, philosophers and politicians, the heroes of Hebrew history have a considerably different background. From a comparison of the two examples comes an uncommon paradigm that still stands before the church today as the example of Kingdom Leadership.

Consistency of The Paradigm

If we were to select a Leadership Hall of Fame from Hebrew history, we would find a very interesting commonality. Let's compare the most prominent leadership personalities—six from the Old Testament and three from the New Testament. These are men who sought after God's heart. They learned to think in a higher way than what made sense to their peers. They were put in front of a nation and expected to lead them in God's direction.

Abraham: Father of a Nation—A Shepherd

Abraham was chosen by God to receive the covenant that would establish the nation of Israel. He was asked to take his family, leave his homeland

and go to a new country. In leading nearly one thousand people to a new land, it was his responsibility to provide direction, daily needs, protection and training (Ge 14:14).[1] Seeing this, it is important to note that Abraham was a shepherd (Ge 13:5). He was a man well acquainted with taking care of the needs of animals that have no capacity to care for themselves.

Joseph: Provider for a Nation—A Shepherd

Joseph was the great grandson of Abraham. He also found himself in a position to lead a nation. He was taken into Egypt as a slave, but was promoted to leadership after showing his ability to get results and to be God's spokesman. God gave him the interpretation of Pharaoh's dream and exalted him to be governor of the land. After serving in the house of Potiphar, then watching the guards in the prison, and then observing the courts of Pharaoh, Joseph had ample experience with Egyptian power-based leadership. When his time came to lead by taking responsibility for preparing for the years of famine, Joseph showed a servant's heart as he assisted Egypt in growing grain, building storage, and planning distribution.

Through Joseph's leadership not only was Egypt saved, but so were other surrounding nations—including Israel. It is important to note that before he was sold into slavery, Joseph was a shepherd (Ge 37:2). He also was acquainted with meeting the needs of helpless animals. He learned even more about being a servant in the house of Potiphar and again in an Egyptian dungeon. In spite of all the harshness, he emerged with a shepherd's heart.

Moses: Deliverer of a Nation—A Shepherd

Like Joseph, Moses began his leadership career in Pharaoh's court where he lived daily with the exploits of power and position. When he first felt the need to do something to lead his people, he tried force, perhaps the only way he knew. In order to retrain the potential in this young man, God led him into the Midian desert to learn a new way of life. He became a shepherd. Moses went from being waited upon to caring for animals that needed to be waited upon. He learned the Shepherd's Paradigm for leadership.

Joshua: General of a Nation – Mentored to be a Shepherd

When it was time for Israel to receive a new leader, their present leader, Moses, prayed a special prayer. "May the Lord provide a man over this community who will think like a shepherd" (Nu 27:15-18). Since he was a young man, Joshua had been an aide to Moses (Nu 11:28), beside him in nearly every conceivable leadership situation. He was a military leader and a spy. He accompanied Moses to Sinai and to the Tent of Meeting for prayer. When it was his time he had learned the Shepherd's Paradigm and led Israel as a shepherd cares for his own.

David: Sovereign of a Nation—A Shepherd

Books have been written about David's leadership. While he was a young shepherd caring for his father's sheep, he was moved to the king's residence to play music to soothe Saul's troubled mind. As he had slain the bear to deliver his sheep from harm, he slew Goliath to deliver Israel. As he had protected his sheep from the lion, he protected Israel from the Philistines. As he found green pastures for his flock, he led Israel to find wealth. Under David's leadership Israel's cup ran over. During his reign they became the strongest nation of their time.

That David had accomplished all this with a heart for God and the leadership paradigm of a shepherd is confirmed in two Scriptures:

> And David shepherded them with integrity of heart; with skillful hands he led them.
> —Ps 78:72

> I will place over them one shepherd, my servant David, and he will tend them; he will tend them and be their shepherd. I the LORD will be their God, and my servant David will be prince among them. I the LORD have spoken.
> —Eze 34:23-24

Nehemiah: Restorer of a Nation—A King's Servant

Nehemiah is the only great Old Testament leader for whom we find no connection to shepherding. However, he was a man who was well acquainted with the meaning of *service*. As a special servant to the king, he was also well acquainted with the words and judgments of power. He was dedicated to what God has put on his heart to do (Ne 2:12). He worked with the people to encourage them and he took his place in building the wall. The wall was built in an amazing amount of time because the people had a heart to work. Their heart was the result of Nehemiah standing with them, encouraging and protecting as a shepherd would his sheep.

Peter: Jewish Evangelist—"Be shepherds of God's Flock." 1 Peter 5:2

Turning to New Testament leaders we find no change in the consistency of the Shepherd Paradigm for leadership. Peter instructed his fellow shepherds to remember the example of the "Chief Shepherd" (1Pe 5:4).

Paul: Gentile Evangelist—"Be shepherds of the church of God." Acts 20:28

Later we will spend an entire chapter on Paul's example of Kingdom Leadership. However, we get a glimpse of the consistency of the Shepherd Paradigm as he met with the elders from the church in Ephesus. His entire conversation with them was bathed in the paradigm of shepherding.

Jesus: Kingdom Authority—"I am the Good Shepherd" John 10:11,14

Jesus, upon whom all authority rested, refused the examples of power-based leadership displayed in Rome and Jerusalem and maintained the consistency of the Shepherd's Paradigm. He announced to his disciples that he was The Good Shepherd and described what that would look like. However, let us look at other Scriptures that confirm the model seen in Jesus.

God promised through the prophets that the Messiah would be one who followed the Shepherd's Paradigm.

> "'But you, Bethlehem, in the land of Judah, are by no means least among the rulers of Judah; for out of you will come a ruler who will be the shepherd of my people Israel.'"
> —Mic 5:2, Mt 2:6

Not only the Messiah would follow this model, God promised Israel that He would send other leaders who followed the Shepherd's Paradigm. "Then I will give you shepherds after my own heart, who will lead you with knowledge and understanding" (Jer 3:15). Note also what is to be the result of God's covenant with His people:

> "May the God of peace, who through the blood of the eternal covenant brought back from the dead our Lord Jesus, that great Shepherd of the sheep."
> —Heb 13:20

Finally, compare the picture of God's rule on earth as it is in heaven:

> He tends his flock like a shepherd: He gathers the lambs in his arms and carries them close to his heart; he gently leads those that have young.
> —Isa 40:11

> "For the Lamb at the center of the throne will be their shepherd; he will lead them to springs of living water. And God will wipe away every tear from their eyes."
> —Rev 7:17

Does this suggest a pattern for biblical leadership? Once again, listen to the words of Jesus in the midst of a world where power, position and authority were the signs of success:

> "You know that those who are regarded as rulers of the Gentiles lord it over them, and their high officials exercise authority over them. Not so with you. Instead, whoever wants to become great among you must be your servant, and whoever wants to be first must be slave of all. For even the Son of Man did not come to be served, but to serve, and to give his life as a ransom for many."
> —Mk 10:41-45

THE CONTRAST OF THE PARADIGM

Jesus' reference to himself as *The Good Shepherd* (Jn 10:11,14) presupposes that there is an opposite, a *Poor Shepherd*. In light of this suggestion we find three passages of Scripture that allow us to contrast good and bad in the eyes of God. To help us further establish the concept of the Shepherd Paradigm, let's compare these three passages to our definition of biblical leadership.

Leadership is Relational

Jesus described the *Good Shepherd* approaching the sheep from the front gate (Jn 10:2). They know him. When he speaks, they recognize his voice (Jn 10:4). In contrast, the *Poor Shepherd* approaches the sheep from the back. The sheep do not know him, and he fears they will not trust him (Jn 10:5). A Good Shepherd knows when a sheep is weak or injured and tends to its needs (Eze 34:13-14). The Poor Shepherd ignores the weak (Eze 34:4). Ezekiel says that this is the case because the Poor Shepherd is too busy taking care of himself (34:8). He simply does not care for the sheep (Jn 10:13).

I once was involved in an exchange of email between one of my teaching colleagues and a man who desired to write a book on leadership success. The author wanted my definition for a successful leader in the modern world. I shared examples of how successful leaders built relationships with their people and kept their needs in mind. The writer continually disagreed. He believed that the only criterion for success was the amount of money the leader made for his company and himself. In his final email to me, he said, "You have no concept of what it means to be a leader, for leaders cannot be responsible for people. Leaders are only responsible for the bottom line." His *common* view of leadership would receive the same response from God as did the shepherds in Ezekiel 34.

Leadership is Service

Peter uses the word *serve* to describe the church leader as a *good shepherd* (1Pe 5:1). In fact, this leader is *eager* to serve (5:3). It is not a duty, but a responsibility. It is God's plan for the shepherd to take care of the flock–see to its needs and make those needs a priority beyond her own (Eze 34:2). In service, good shepherds search out good pasture for the sheep and lead them there (Eze 34:13).

In contrast, poor shepherds look out only for self (Eze 34:2). Peter observes that they love money (5:3) and have a tendency to lord it over their people (5:3). Although he does not use the word *shepherd,* Jesus makes a scathing statement about those who consider themselves religious leaders. Please allow me to paraphrase Jesus' statement with a modern application that I have witnessed all around the world.

> Beware of the *poor shepherds*. They like to walk around in expensive suits and haircuts. They love to be greeted in the marketplaces (especially by other people of importance) and demand to have the most important seats in the church service and the places of honor at meetings and meals. They take financial advantage of their own people and for a show make loud and lengthy prayers. Such men will be punished most severely.
> —Author's paraphrase of Luke 20:46-47

Leadership is Dedicated

The good shepherd is dedicated to the point that he is willing to die for the protection of the sheep, while the poor shepherd runs at the slightest sign of trouble. However, the dedication is not only to the point of death; it is a willing (1Pe 5:2), daily ministry committed to the needs of the sheep. If a lamb strays away, the good shepherd looks for it. In contrast, the poor shepherd will ignore the stray (Lk 15:4-6, Eze 34:5,8). With little thought for himself, the good shepherd is dedicated to the needs of his sheep. A poor shepherd is dedicated to self-promotion. A good shepherd is dedicated to the success of others.

Leadership is Assistance

If a sheep is hurt, the shepherd tends to its needs (Eze 34:15). If one is weak, the shepherd strengthens it (Eze 34:16). In contrast, the poor shepherd is so concentrated on self-interest and personal desires that he does not have time to spend taking care of foolish sheep who get themselves hurt or who become weak.

A leadership trainer from the nation of Taiwan tells a story that sums up the contrast between the good shepherd and bad shepherd.

> The spectacle of an eastern shepherd going ahead of his sheep is still a common sight in Israel today. An Arab guide was once showing a group of tourists around the Holy Land. On one of their coach trips, he alluded to this tradition of the Palestinian shepherd walking in front of his flock. While he was speaking, the tourists spotted a man in the distance driving a small flock of sheep with a rather menacing stick. Just as all schoolchildren love to prove their teachers wrong, they pointed the figure to the guide.
>
> He immediately stopped the bus and rushed off across the fields. A few minutes later he returned, his face beaming. He announced, "I have just spoken to the man. Ladies and gentlemen, he is not the shepherd. He is in fact the butcher!"[2]

THE APPLICATION OF THE PARADIGM

God meant for us to find our leadership paradigm in the heart of the shepherd. There we will find the example of service that produces true followers. Power-based leaders will always have to protect their position and control the thinking and actions of followers. This, because there will always be someone seeking to dethrone them. By the way of contrast, servant leaders, drawing on the shepherd paradigm, concentrate on the needs of the sheep—being devoted to serving, assisting, nourishing, and protecting. In return, the sheep willingly follow and provide for the leader's needs. Seeking to give a blessing, the servant leader accepts responsibility and shuns demonstrations of authority.

Into a world where position, power and control were the highest goals, came a Carpenter from Nazareth. Jesus, at the height of his popularity, gave the finest example of true leadership. Knowing "that the Father had put all things under his power, and that he had come from God and was returning to God," (Jn 13:3) he stripped his clothes to the waist and girded himself with a towel to stoop to wash the feet of His followers. Having performed the duties of the lowliest of servants, he said, "I have set you an example that you should do as I have done for you" (Jn 13:15).

CHAPTER FIVE

UNCOMMON STRATEGY

"He has made us competent as ministers of a new covenant—not of the letter but of the Spirit; for the letter kills, but the Spirit gives life."
—2 Corinthians 3:6

"For this reason Christ is the mediator of a new covenant, that those who are called may receive the promised eternal inheritance."
—Hebrews 9:15

It was not long after the arrival of the new staff member that we discovered that he did not have the teaching or personal skills for the job. His professors and people who knew him had assured us that he was the man we needed. However, there were some serious deficiencies. We were faced with a decision; "do we pack him up and send him home, or do we work with him to help him become the person everyone believed he could be?" We chose the second option.

I contacted a person in our town who was nationally known to have abilities in this area of ministry. We outlined a six-month teaching program for the young man. I sat down with our new staff member and said, "We want you to stay and become an effective leader in your area. Therefore, we are offering you the following covenant. If you will meet with the chosen mentor, study the curriculum the mentor makes available, and spend time observing others who are in your same area of ministry, we will continue our relationship to you and provide for your continued growth in ministry." The young man accepted the covenant agreement.

When God summoned Israel's leaders to Mount Sinai, He was well aware that they were new at leadership in a free environment. He realized they needed direction. Therefore, instead of commanding them or negotiating a contract, God offered Israel's leadership a *covenant*. They were told, "If you obey me fully and keep my covenant, then out of all nations you will be my treasured possession. Although the whole earth is mine, you will be for me a kingdom of priests and a holy nation" (Ex 19:5-6). When Moses presented the covenant to the leaders, they pledged, "Everything the Lord has said we will do" (Ex 24:3).

The leadership relationship that God had with Israel was just as uncommon in Moses' day as it is today. Plato and Aristotle did not create a strategy of "leadership power, suppression and servitude;" however, they defined what was common and made it academically and philosophically acceptable. One modern author describes the common as thinking "in terms of formal authority, position, status ... control, command, coerce, dominate, govern, or manipulate."[1] God has never been accountable to man's common thinking. His dealings with Israel show another example of His higher way of thinking, higher way of action. Stephen Covey says that true leadership thinking is "a better way, a higher way."[2]

In the Old Testament the Hebrew word *chesed* is used more than any other to describe God's character. Over 150 times this word is used in connection with the way God acts toward people. The root of the Hebrew word is the verb, *to follow through*. The literal translation of *chesed* is *covenant keeper*. Dr. Mont Smith defines *chesed* as "faithfulness to an oath ... acting in such a way that the other is benefited."[3]

Most Bible scholars do not use the literal *covenant keeper* when translating the Scripture. Therefore, we do not find the words, *covenant keeper* as descriptive of God in most translations. When translators of Scripture find a word that is difficult to interpret literally, they search for what is known as the dynamic equivalent, or the word in the language and culture that best restates the concept of the original word. In most languages the equivalents are *faith-*

ful, faithfulness, mercy, merciful, loving kindness and *everlasting love.*

God's strategy from Genesis to Revelation has been to work with His people on the basis of covenants. Smith writes, "The idea of covenant is inseparably connected to every major idea in the Bible."[4] It becomes the common in God's uncommon.

Based on the Hebrew word *berith* ("to bind together"), Biblical covenants are agreements between God and His people that will bring blessing to both Himself and those who choose to take part. All covenants have a statement of terms (what must be done to fulfill the agreement) and promises (what the person entering the agreement will receive for fulfilling the terms). Scriptural covenants are fairly easy to spot by noticing combinations of words such as, "I will ... if you will ..."

The study of biblical covenants reveals two consistent points. First, God's commitment to bless

---

IMPORTANT COVENANTS OF SCRIPTURE

(Notice the terms and promises)

Covenant with Abraham: The LORD had said to Abram, "**[if you]** Leave your country, your people and your father's household and go to the land **I will** show you, **I will** ... bless you." (Ge 12:1-3).

Covenant with David: The LORD swore an oath to David, a sure oath that He will not revoke:

> "One of your own descendants **I will** place on your throne. **If your sons** keep my covenant and the statutes I teach them, then their sons **will sit** on your throne for ever and ever." (Ps 132:11-12).

those who accept the terms of His covenant. Second, over 150 times God is referred to by biblical authors as *chesed* (covenant keeper). We discover that God is committed to following through on what He promises. According to Smith, the core meaning of *chesed* is "faithfulness to commitments and to legitimate expectations."[5] However, what sets a covenant apart from other types of agreements is that within the covenant is a commitment to strengthen and meet the needs of both parties. In other words, both the individuals making the covenant and those entering into it will be blessed.

What does a study of covenant mean to our uncommon leadership strategy? First, it gives another insight into God's heart (His desire to have a people to bless), thereby providing another picture of what it means to have a "heart for God." Second, it explains that God is looking for leaders whose focus is on serving others in ways that bring blessing to both parties. Covenant leadership is taking action that goes beyond words to following through on a commitment to help people grow.

> "Covenantal leadership is taking the responsibility to provide and maintain an atmosphere that promotes the best for both leader and follower."

Jesus made it very clear that He came to *serve* (Mt 20:28). Everywhere He turned in His ministry people were blessed, either through teaching or through touch (sometimes both). He was not too busy to bless children. He was not too proud to wash feet. He ministered to the rich, the poor, the elite and the outcasts. All these were blessed as He fulfilled the promise made by His Father.

> The Spirit of the Sovereign LORD is on me, because the LORD has anointed me to preach good news to the poor. He has sent me to bind up the brokenhearted, to proclaim freedom for the captives and release from darkness for the prisoners, to proclaim the year of the LORD'S favor and the day of vengeance of our God, to comfort all who mourn...
>
> —Isa 61:1-2

In light of this, we must assume that the Kingdom Strategy is for leaders to be trustworthy in their commitment to serve people. As with God, they can be depended upon to follow through with character and action in such a way that those who follow have a sense of security. Another author uses the words, "integrity",[6] "trust"[7] and a "relationship of genuine courtesy, respect, and appreciation for the other person"[8] to describe a trustworthy leader.

The Apostle Paul worked to equip people for service so they and the church could be stronger (Eph 4:12). He wanted to bring Christians together in unity so that all would be blessed (Col 2:2). Another Christian author and famous American corporate leader says that covenant relationships "reflect unity and grace."[9] Covenants free people to grow. They do not separate or dominate people.

Therefore, the Kingdom Strategy is not to rule people with harshness and control. It is to follow the uncommon example seen in God's dealing with His people. It is seen in Jesus' focus of ministry. It is modeled in the ministry of Paul. Covenant Leaders take responsibility in such a way that both leader and follower find God's fulfillment. The leader's desire is to promote what is best for others.

Leaders have three basic tools available to them. The following chart shows a comparison.

A common tool used in leadership is the command. By using a command, a leader uses his position of authority to dictate what the servant must

Leadership Tools Chart

	COMMAND	CONTRACT	COVENANT
PARTIES	Authority & Servant	Authority & Receiver	Authority & Receiver
TERMS	Dictated	Negotiated	Presented
PROMISES	Dictated	Negotiated	Presented
PURPOSE	Accomplish Task	Protect Parties	Bless Parties

do. The servant must then obey or receive the consequences. The purpose of a command is usually to accomplish a task that the commander wants done. Command is a valid tool in a military situation or where emergency workers are embroiled in rescue and ensuring peace. However, one has to question its validity outside these realms.

A contract is a transaction between the person in authority and those who will be fulfilling the negotiated terms. It is made by getting both parties to compromise their demands. The purpose of a contract is to protect both parties so that, if one should breach its contract, the other will have a position before a court of law. In labor disputes and financial agreements, *contracts* seem to be a necessity for our day. However, there are some great leaders of Western industry who never had a contract with their people. Instead, they used the third tool available to leaders.

A covenant is a blend of the other two tools. It is a listing of terms and promises that are set forth by the one in authority. In the formation of the terms and promises the leader attempts to address the needs of people and promote what is best for them. The receiver then has the option to choose to be in or out of the covenant. The principle that makes a covenant work is the follow-through. If both parties are faithful to the covenant, then both are blessed. We will see in a later chapter in this study that all of the words that describe the Kingdom Strategy are words that are based in serving needs. A covenantal

Uncommon Strategy

leader is one who listens to and cares for the needs of his/her people. Such a leader bases the covenant on meeting those needs while fulfilling the needs of the organization.

The focus of the Kingdom Strategy is then to participate in a ministry that blesses people. The Kingdom Strategy is not concerned with positions, titles or power. It is concerned about people growing and finding the abundance of life that Jesus promised (Jn 10:10). Covenant leaders create relationships that "induce freedom, not paralysis."[10] The goal of leadership is "to make people feel stronger."[11] Leaders must "create systems that support growth."[12]

There is, however, what I call the backside to the covenant. One of the common misconceptions about the subject of servant leadership is that the leader must allow people to make all the decisions. Those who misunderstand think that leaders become waiters upon those in their care and must bow to their every whim. There could be nothing further from the truth. Kingdom Leaders are not weak. In fact it takes more strength to be a servant-based leader than it does to stand on a power-base. Servant-based leadership maintains a "balance between courage and consideration."[13]

When God established the covenant with Israel, He gave a long list of the blessing that Israel would enjoy (Dt 28:1-14). One would wonder upon reading this list how anyone would ever turn their backs on such an offering. However, God went on to warn that if they did walk away from the covenant, the blessing would not be there. In fact, with their removal of themselves from the covenant, a list of curses would replace the blessings (Dt 28:15-68). It was not a matter so much of God sending punishment as it was Israel walking away from His blessing.

I wish I could report that all ended well in my covenant with the young man who came to be on our church staff. However, even though he accepted the agreement, he never called the mentor, neither did he study any of the curriculum nor did he observe any other leaders. Twice I renewed the covenant with him and encouraged him to get started. At the end of the appointed period he was dismissed from the church.

History would like to record that all ended well in God's covenant with Israel. However, even though Israel had accepted the agreement, they had a very difficult time following the leaders God had provided. God continually warned them and renewed the covenant with them. Nevertheless, God came to the point where it was obvious that Israel had no interest in fulfilling its part of the covenant. Therefore, God sent His son to offer a new covenant to a new people.

> When Israel continually ignored the covenant, God said: "The time is coming, declares the Lord, when I will make a new covenant with the house of Israel and with the house of Judah. It will not be like the covenant I made with their forefathers

when I took them by the hand to lead them out of Egypt, because they did not remain faithful to my covenant, and I turned away from them, declares the Lord."

—Heb 8:8-9

The purpose of the Kingdom Strategy is to lead in such ways that people are blessed. They are free to grow and become what God designed for them to be. The covenant leader stands ready to fulfill his or her promises. However, if people refuse to follow, they walk away from the blessings offered in the covenant. If, after trying to retrieve them they continue to walk away, the leader must allow them to go.

In my experience, one of the greatest joys of leadership is to see people grow. I liken it to the blooming of a flower. And this is the purpose behind biblical leadership strategy—to cause the blooming of potential leaders. This can only be accomplished through a relationship of leader to learner that allows both to grow. The satisfaction comes as you observe the learner becoming an effective leader.

CHAPTER SIX

UNCOMMON TESTING

They must first be tested; and then if there is nothing against them, let them serve as deacons.
—1 Timothy 3:10

River Convergence

On our first trip to Myanmar I stood on the banks of the great Ayeyarwady River and marveled at its size. I get the same feeling of awe when I stand beside America's Mississippi River or the great Zambezi that flows through Zambia and Mozambique. There is such grandeur in the flow of these waterways. Where have their waters come from? If the river could speak, what would it tell me? Whose lives were touched as the river passed through the land? What crops were nourished by its flow?

When I stand on the bank of a mighty river, I tend to believe that all the way up, beyond where I can see, this river has always been this size. In Egypt we followed the River Nile for over a hundred miles and never saw a change in its size. Surely it began as a mighty river, didn't it? I don't often stop to think that somewhere there is a beginning. There is a place where small streams of water form creeks, and creeks join to become small rivers, and small rivers merge into larger rivers until their waters join to become the seemingly unstoppable flow before me. I do not think about the obstacles that it had to overcome or circumvent in its beginning stages.

The birth and growth of a mighty river is a story to be told. But so is the birth and growth of every leader. I am sometimes guilty, however, of looking at the work of a powerful man or woman of God and having the same thoughts as when I view the river. I see the strength of their life and marvel at their confidence in Christ. I hear them share words of wisdom that I long to be able to think for myself. I convince myself that I could never be like them.

It is easy to make the mistake of thinking that a strong leader has always been a strong leader. I assume that this person was born with these experiences and this wisdom. I don't stop to think that somewhere in the younger years of his life there was a beginning. There were many wrong decisions and failed attempts. Each had to sit at the feet of a master to learn. I need to be reminded that the spiritual wisdom I admire comes from hours of study, and then applying that study to difficult, even tragic life situations. Perhaps if I searched I would find times when they, like Elijah, just quit, thinking they were alone and the job was much too difficult (1Ki 19:14). But, like the mighty river, Elijah overcame obstacles, rolling on wiser, stronger and more determined than ever. So does the effective leader today.

Leaders are not born to be leaders. Their lives are formed as the many streams of experience flow together to create the leader we see. They are men and women who made a conscious choice to allow the streams of life to converge into service to others. For this reason, *service* and *dedicated* appear in the definition of leadership. Leadership is a decision to answer God's call to stand in the gap (Eze 22:30) and fill a need that will result in God's people being blessed. To do that, one must have an uncommonly dedicated servant's heart.

There are often years of preparation that take place before God's call. There are miles of streams converging before they become what we know as the *mighty river*. There is no mention of how many years transpired between Joseph being sold into slavery and being made governor of Egypt. We know that at least eighty years went into preparing Moses (forty in Egypt and forty in Midian) to lead Israel. Joshua worked over forty years as Moses' aide before he became the leader of Israel. There were at least fourteen years between Paul's conversion and his first missionary journey (Gal 2:1). During these periods there were many lessons and experiences converging to prepare the mighty servants we know in Scripture.

We grow through the streams of testing that God allows into our lives. They mold us according to His design. The Scriptures record that God tested Abraham (Ge 22), Gideon (Jdg 6-7) and Job (Job 23:10). David was tested as Saul pursued him through the deserts. Jesus was tested in the wilderness (Mt 4:1). Paul wrote that a person who is appointed as a deacon "must first be tested" (1Ti 3:8).

Paul was a man "approved by God" (1Th 2:4). Peter taught that our "faith may be proved genuine and may result in praise" (1Pe 1:7). Peter's second letter adds that the trials we endure "will keep [us] from being ineffective and unproductive in [our] knowledge of our Lord Jesus Christ" (2Pe 1:8-9).

I once watched a man making a beautiful stone that was to be set in a ring. He began with a piece of coarse unattractive rock, which I would have passed over or tossed away. However, the man's trained eye knew its potential. I watched as he sliced the rock and examined its layers. He marked a shape on one of the slices and cut some more. As I watched I started imagining, *What if that rock could cry out? Would it plead for him to stop?*

Then the jeweler took the shaped piece and went to a special grinding machine that had seven different grinding wheels ranging from coarse to smooth. Again I imagined the stone crying out, "Please stop! That hurts!" Nevertheless, the designer continued until his work resulted in a beautiful stone that was set in a silver ring that I still own. Now I look at it and think, "If this stone had known it was to become so beautiful in its final form, it would have joyfully endured the testing."

God has a design for our lives and he knows what needs to be done to shape us for that cause. For some the time of shaping will be short. For others it will be a long journey. At times in our lives we will cry out to God, "Please stop! That hurts!" Still, because He has in mind the final result, He will, in love, continue to shape us for the task. It is only those who keep themselves in the hands of the Master who become a mighty river or a beautiful gemstone.

There are many areas in which a leader can be tested. These are the streams that make one great river. I want to suggest three streams that converge to create the core of any leader. Just as a river never stops receiving water, there is no age at which a leader's testing begins or ends. There are no limits on the severity of each test. However, the final product will perfectly fit the task assigned to the leader.

THE STREAMS OF HERITAGE

The Psalmist declares that we were "knit together" in our mother's womb (Ps 139:13-16). He said that God knew what our body would be like and what would transpire during our days. God knew our parents and birthplace. He knew the type of home we were being brought into. He knew the value system by which our parents would raise us. He designed us for a purpose. However, not everyone appreciates the design.

These components are what we refer to when we talk about our *heritage*. They are circumstances and events of our birth over which we have no control. We do not choose our parents, our ethnic or tribal identity, our shape, our abilities or our economic position. However, we must respond to them. We choose whether we will accept God's design or rebel against it. These components are all small tributaries that create the river's flow.

I have met many people who were angry with God as a designer. They believe they were born to the wrong parents in the wrong country. They curse their situation and refuse to accept that God could be a loving God and "do this to them." They claim they could be successful "if only God had made them taller." "If only God had given me musical ability." "If only I were born into a different family." For some, these elements of design become a test as they are ridiculed or teased about physical characteristics—a handicap, birthmark or body size. This testing can be especially strong in the developmental years of childhood. They become angry and/or depressed concerning the circumstances over which they have no control. They believe that "if only" certain things in their life had been different, they would be able to serve more effectively.

Uncommon Testing

In nearly every country where we teach, we see people who were given difficult circumstances to overcome. Some are sitting on street corners holding out their hands hoping people will feel sorry for their condition and give them a coin. Others, however, have passed the test and overcome. One such man is an evangelist in Zimbabwe who was stricken with polio at the age of two that left him without the use of one leg. His parents didn't want him to go to school or train for a job. He persevered and has led in planting over two hundred churches in four countries. We know an evangelist in Thailand who also suffered polio as a youth. He is unable to walk but still holds evangelistic campaigns in the mountain villages of his country. A young lady in Honduras has overcome abandonment by her father, abuse by a relative, and third degree burns over one-third of her body. She now shares the gospel with teens who have experienced similar trauma.

Leaders who pass the heritage test are those who accept God's design and seek ways to use it for His glory. I used to spend a lot of time being upset about not having musical ability. At times I was angry with God. I spent a lot of energy trying to develop as a musician. When I finally accepted the fact that music was not in God's design for me, I was able to develop in the areas that God had gifted in me. When I was able to relax and allow God's design to be worked in my life, I found much joy.

God's design of our heritage has a purpose that will be used to write a story of ministry in His Kingdom. People who accept God's design will, like the jeweler's stone, become an object of beauty in the eye of the Designer. Those who reject the heritage God has set will never be able to serve with the joy and effectiveness that He desires for us.

STREAMS OF CHARACTER

As was mentioned in the chapter on Uncommon Measurements, character is the most important ingredient in Christian leadership. God is looking for men and women who have His heart. That heart is partly demonstrated in one's character. Therefore, God will allow experiences to flow into our life that will build our reputation in the eyes of others so that we can share His message.

We must remember that Satan came into the Garden of Eden to tempt Adam and Eve to turn from God's plan to accept a plan that seemed right. Believers can expect similar temptations to which they must respond. The response to each decision builds the character and reputation we will hold before our people.

The English word *character* has its beginning in the history of printing. A printer would carve a letter or mark to be applied to the page. This mark was known as an engraving and would be used many times. When the printer picked up the engraved piece, he knew where it would be used by the character etched on it. The word later was used to describe the morals and values by which a person was known, those characteristics etched on his life.[1]

Uncommon Testing

There is no specific age at which character begins to be etched. Scriptures do not reveal a curriculum that must be passed so that character growth will take place. There is no point at which we can declare that we have passed.

Some Christians will grow through these tests, and others will not. There are no easy trails to maturity. Failure will come to those who try to find a shortcut to avoid testing. The secular philosophies provide many shortcuts. All we have to do is tell a few lies or manipulate our way. Perhaps stealing will solve life's problem. Some think that just one or two trips with drugs will put them in a position to have money and, therefore, more respect. However, those who travel the mountain trails know that cutting a new shorter trail has many dangers—snakes, quicksand or other unknowns can bring pain or death. So it is with trying to take the shorter ways in life development.

As a Christian grows in Christ, he or she will encounter different types of experiences that will converge to build strong character and provide credibility when speaking on Biblical themes. Let's mention three of these experiences.

1. Experiences that test honor

Honor is a reputation for being true to what we say. I define it as "standing consistent in what we claim to believe." People lose honor, or *face,* when their actions reveal that they are not what they profess. The English word most used for the concept of honor is *integrity*. This word comes from a Latin word that means *whole, undivided* or *complete*.[2] It is used to describe a person who shows the same character in all circumstances.

The Scriptures speak of *righteousness*. Good character is part of that righteousness. David gives one definition of his understanding of righteousness, or integrity, by defining who has the character to dwell in God's sanctuary.

> LORD, who may dwell in your sanctuary?
>   Who may live on your holy hill?
> He whose walk is blameless
>   and who does what is righteous,
> who speaks the truth from his heart
>   and has no slander on his tongue,
> who does his neighbor no wrong
>   and casts no slur on his fellowman,
> who despises a vile man
>   but honors those who fear the LORD,
> who keeps his oath
>   even when it hurts,
> who lends his money without usury
>   and does not accept a bribe against the innocent.
> He who does these things
>   will never be shaken.
>
> —Ps 15: 1-5

Uncommon Testing

Honor develops as others recognize that a person possesses the same distinguishing marks of character whether they are at home, in church or in the village. Such a person is *whole,* living a life that is not divided into parts (home, work and/or village life).

I shall never forget the day that the seventeen-year-old daughter of a church elder approached me with a shocking announcement. In American culture and law, when children turn eighteen they are no longer considered to be the responsibility of their parents. This girl told me, "Next month I will be eighteen, and you will never see me in church again." When I asked her why, she responded, "You know my father at church. I know him at home. He is not the same person." This man, in fact, was a husband, father, church elder, business owner and mayor of our town. In each role he showed different values. I discovered that at home he was known for his anger and vulgar language. The church people knew him as a fine Christian. In the town he was known for his dishonesty. The man lacked integrity. His life was lived in *parts*. He was not a man of honor.

When my son was the youth pastor of a large church. He once had a chance to talk to the son of the senior pastor—the man who led the church and preached every week. My son asked the pastor's son, "What is it like to live with this man?" The pastor's son answered, "The man you see in the pulpit is the same man I see at home." Wherever this man was, he was known for the same values. He lived what he preached. This Christian leader has integrity. His life is whole. He is a man of honor. God's strong leaders are those who pass the tests of character and remain whole.

2. Experiences that test obedience to God

Obedience must be learned before it can be taught. Our character in the eyes of God is built as He reveals His truth and direction and we obey. This test is "a process through which a leader learns to recognize, understand, and obey God's voice."[3] A parent who constantly breaks the law cannot expect children to be model citizens. A youth pastor who rebels against authority will have a difficult time teaching teens to obey.

When God sent Moses to deliver the people from Egypt he was told to take the entire nation on a three-day journey to offer sacrifices (Ex 8:7). Pharaoh offered him many partial solutions—sacrifice here in Egypt (Ex 8:25), take only the men (Ex 10:11), take the women but leave the livestock (Ex 10:24). Moses could have accepted any of these offers, but would that have been obedience?

Daniel was well aware of the food laws that God had given to keep His people healthy and strong. When the king offered him the "best of his kitchen" (Da 1:8), Daniel could have rationalized, "But, I was commanded by the king." However, would that have been obedience to all that God wanted? Instead, he offered the king an alternative that would fulfill his goal and maintain Daniel's obedience to God (Da 1:12-13). Daniel passed the test and went on to become a great leader among the Babylonians as well as among God's people.

I once worked with a youth pastor who was caught in sexual sin. I was so angry with him I did not even want to talk to him. The next morning I opened the Bible for my devotions and the Scripture for that morning was, "Brothers, if someone is caught in a sin, you who are spiritual should restore him gently. But watch yourself, or you also may be tempted" (Gal 6:1).

I was angry. My thoughts had nothing to do with restoring him gently. I defiantly said, "I am not going to do it!" I sat in my chair for several minutes, fuming, and then finally decided to obey. That night I shared with the elders and we made a plan to restore the young man to Christ. God did not give us Scripture for us to compromise. He knows what is best and only through obedience will we experience His best.

3. Experiences that develop maturity

Earlier in this chapter I told about the jeweler making the stone for my ring. The final polishing of the stone is one of the most critical steps. The potential of the stone was recognized and its value was growing with each step the jeweler took. However, there remained some waste to be trimmed or some imperfection to be smoothed. At this point the gemstone will either polish or break. If it shatters, the stone will be worth far less than first thought. If it withstands the test, it will shine to its potential.

Mature character develops through hardship, trial and difficulty. "God does not stop working on character after moving someone into leadership. God continues to form character throughout the life of a leader."[4] In order to mature our leadership He will allow certain experiences into our life to make our leadership stronger. If we withstand the pressure, we become the leaders He foresaw. If we break, our leadership will suffer.

My second ministry took place in a church that was large and prestigious. I really believed that because they had chosen me to be their pastor I was on my way to being a famous pastor. I would be asked to speak at conventions. People would come to me for advice on how to be successful. That all came to an end half way through my second year when the elders called me to a meeting to tell me that my ministry was being terminated. I was shaken to my roots. I questioned God. I blamed the leaders for not recognizing my worth. I screamed at everyone but me.

God wasn't done with me until two years later during my next ministry. I was still blaming others for my failure. Even though I screamed at Him to stop, God patiently worked me on the polishing wheel. Finally I realized that I had been the root of the problem. My concepts of leadership were far from what Scripture revealed. God used a conference, which I reluctantly attended, and the first book I had ever read on the subject of leadership[5] to begin the process of helping me realize He had a different plan for my life. I surrendered. Now God could use me. Clinton writes,

> If a leader refuses to see the hand of God in this intense processing, but instead blames circumstances or people, or rationalizes away the processing, then [God's objective] may not develop.[6]

After studying the lives of some of the greatest Christian leaders—the mighty rivers of leadership, the gemstones of God's history—men such as Wilbur Chapman, D.L. Moody, Hudson Taylor, Isaac Watt, F.B. Meyer, and William Mueller, Robert Clinton writes,

> The average for these [leaders] was fifteen years after they entered their life work before they began to know the Lord Jesus as their Life, and ceased trying to work for Him and began allowing Him to be their all in all and do His work through them.[7]

STREAMS OF LEADERSHIP

The final streams of testing to which each of us will be exposed are those tests that confirm our ability to do the work of leadership. The tests for this are likely to be small at first. However, as one becomes faithful in small tasks, God allows larger areas of responsibility. We must beware of our own expectations that we will immediately be as strong and important as those who have been serving for years. Even the mightiest river began as a small stream.

For most, the first streams of leadership testing will evaluate us as followers. We cannot be an adequate leader if we do not understand following. Notice that the great leaders of the First Century church were first called to be followers. "Come, follow me," Jesus said, "and I will make you fishers of men." At once they left their nets and followed him (Mt 4:19-20).

Peter reminded the Jewish Christians that they were first to be followers. To this you were called, because Christ suffered for you, leaving you an example that you should follow in his steps (1Pe 2:21).

Once we have proved our faithfulness in following, God will allow us to take responsibility for small areas of leadership. At first the assigned task might seem inconsequential to the emerging leader.

One of the problems being faced in common leadership philosophy is the emphasis on size and personal importance. Power-based thinking requires size and status as the indicators of success. This causes young emerging leaders to believe that they should start with a major responsibility. They get angry when asked to do menial tasks or serve in a small insignificant location. A professor in an American

Bible college to me that many students only want to talk about serving in a large church and getting a good salary. Small churches are considered a lesser ministry. These young leaders believe they should begin as a large river without the small streams.

However, the emerging leader who will mature into God's design will accept the small responsibilities and give his heart to them. To the faithful, more and more streams will come to feed the growing river of their life. As Jesus told the faithful servant, "You have been faithful with a few things; I will put you in charge of many things" (Mt 25:21).

Convergence

Many potential leaders never get this far. They either fail the tests or choose not to participate. Each test builds on the experience of those before it and prepares us for the next. When the rivers of our life are allowed to flow together, we become the river of God's design.

Not long after I had accepted the call to lead my fourth church, I was able to look back into my life and see all the streams coming together. My life experiences, ministry experience, roles, and giftedness all came together. Where my earlier ministries were short and sometimes painful learning experiences, they converged to give me seventeen years of effective leadership in this new leadership responsibility.

Convergence brings with it a new level of leadership power. This is the power of purpose. People who have allowed the events and tests of life to converge are people who "have encountered themselves head on. And they are finding their inner truth, a life purpose, a moral imperative that goes beyond themselves."[8] Those who have grown to this point are now practicing uncommon leadership as they begin to see leadership as "giving away power, allowing others to lead."[9] They realize that they do not have to be in power to make a difference.

When we see a mighty river flowing unhindered, we are awestruck by its power. Rather than the destructive power of a raging river, we see calmness as the waters flow to nourish land, allow commerce, and grant recreation to those touched by its life. The same is true with Kingdom Leaders who have matured according to God's uncommon way of acting and thinking. They flow strong in character and abilities. Leadership is no longer self-centered but now focused on those whose lives can be touched by God's plan. Their goal is "to empower others: to raise them up, love them, give them responsibility, trust them, learn from them, and be led by them."[10] As Clinton concludes, "Unless we experience God's ongoing development we will not be able to help others develop their leadership capacity."[11]

Testing is seldom seen as desirable. Most tests are inconvenient, difficult and sometimes painful. The mighty river has flowed past all the rocks and fallen trees. The gemstone has endured the cutting and the polishing. The strong Kingdom Leader has allowed God to make her into His design.

CHAPTER SEVEN

UNCOMMON AUTHORITY

"All authority in heaven and on earth has been given to [Jesus]. Therefore…"
—Matthew 28:18

There is possibly no subject more misunderstood or where Scripture is misapplied than the biblical teaching concerning *power* and *authority*. The Greek philosophy of leadership was based on the use of power. Jesus brought a new definition and example of leadership for the Kingdom. Unfortunately, shortly after his death, church leaders were pulled back into the allures of power.

Jesus, knowing the problems created by power-based hierarchy, had purposely avoided creating such a structure for the church.

In all His preparation of the twelve disciples, Jesus never emphasized any continuing organization. Nor did the heart of His teaching convey any single verbal formula. When He was betrayed, Jesus prayed that His disciples might be one and that all those who were to believe in Him through their word might be one. While this certainly implied a close and continuing fellowship, it hardly specified any visible structure.[1]

Paul also avoided the creation of a church leadership structure. Having been raised in the Roman culture, he was very well aware of the functions of a "chain-of-command." Yet he avoided titles and discussions concerning his authority (2Co 10:8). In none of his letters to young leaders or to developing churches does he discuss a structure for church authority.[2]

Within one hundred years of the ascension of Christ, the church was completely restructured according to the common patterns of secular philosophy. It looked more like the political systems of the Roman Senate and the Jewish Sanhedrin[3] than the "everyone-is-a-servant" teaching of Jesus, The Cornerstone. The church became like "the rulers of the Gentiles and those in authority," exactly what Jesus had told them they were not to become (Mt 20:25-28; Mk 10:42-43; Lk 22:24-30). Early in the Second Century BC, Ignatius, a leader in the church at Antioch, wrote a series of letters to the churches. Historian Bruce Shelley summarizes Ignatius' writings:

He speaks habitually of a single bishop in each church, a body of presbyters and a company of deacons. God's grace and the Spirit's power flow to the flock through this united ministry.[4]

Latourette, explains what happened next.

The bishops [became] the representative of God the Father and the presbyters are the Sanhedrin of God ... Nothing was done without the bishop ... [Ignatius stated] that he who honors the bishop shall be honored by God."[5]

Rinehart explains the results.

Whether consciously or unconsciously, they began to lead and structure according to the same pattern of the pagan religions that surrounded them. A class of priests held power over the spiritual well being of those under their charge. The worship became increasingly formulaic, with decreasing participation by believers. Leaders adopted a distinctive style of dress and claimed special rights—the ability to grant forgiveness, to withhold the Lord's Supper and to teach the Scriptures. As the clergy class became more defined, the casual observer may well, at times, have mistaken the church for just another mystery cult.[6]

The church, structured in pagan power-based philosophy, sent missionaries to far countries with the good motive of sharing the message of Jesus

Christ. However, they established churches according to the power-based structure of their sending body. When they translated the Bible, they chose words in line with their power-based theology rather than servant-based wording of Scripture.[7] This includes the English King James Version, which translates Greek words for *leader* as *ruler*. (Whatever word is chosen, its application must be measured to Jesus, The Cornerstone.)[8]

This preoccupation with power and authority has existed since Satan tempted Adam and Eve to display the power of their choice in the Garden. Since then people have engaged in all kinds of power struggles: master against slave, pastor against elder, husband against wife, child against parent, student against teacher, rebel against government. One author describes the problem.

> We search eagerly for leadership yet seek to cage and tame it. We recoil from power yet we are bewitched or titillated by it. We devour books on power -- power in the office, power in the bedroom, power in the corridors. Connoisseurs of power purport to teach about it -- what it is, how to get it, how to use it, how to "gain total control" over "everything around you."[9]

In our study of leadership, we must recognize and admit that a foundational point is understanding and deciding about the use of power. We have a decision to make. "Power can be used either to dominate [others] and make them weak, or to uplift [them] and build their competence and self-esteem."[10]

Uncommon Authority

The fourth chapter of Luke begins with Satan's temptation of Jesus in the wilderness (Lk 4:1-13). This exchange provides the basis for an interesting study on the issue of power and authority in the Kingdom of God. Note especially the second temptation and what Satan offered Jesus. If Jesus would just bow down and worship him, Satan offered him *authority* and *splendor* (4:6). Jesus turned him down, saying that we should only worship God. However, perhaps there is another reason—the fact that Jesus already had more authority than Satan had to offer.

According to Luke, after Jesus left the wilderness, he went to Nazareth to announce the beginning of his ministry (4:14-31). He then went to Capernaum where people were astounded as they listened to him teach. The reason for the astonishment is explained, "Because he taught as one having authority" (4:32).

Later, the people were amazed again when they witnessed Jesus' ability to command demons. Matthew records that they were so dumbfounded by his power over evil spirits they asked, "By what authority do you do this?" (4:36). This is interesting when we realize over whom Jesus was displaying authority when he cast out demons—the one who was offering Him all authority.

Jesus demonstrated authority once again; for a third time the people walked away talking to themselves (Lk 5:24). On this occasion, Jesus claimed authority over sin, and they were left wondering, "Who is this man? Only God can forgive sin." Jesus had clearly confirmed his *authority* over what they believed made the man a cripple.

In every act of ministry Jesus demonstrated his *authority*. In light of leadership (power) struggles we experience today, I think it would be good for us to compare the description of Jesus' authority with that of modern church leaders. Let us examine three words that describe Christ's authority as head of the Church.

APPOINTED AUTHORITY:
EXOUSIA = "AUTHORITY CONFERRED BY A HIGHER AUTHORITY."

Exousia is the most common word for authority used in the New Testament. It is usually used to describe the authority of a civil leader: "Someone put in charge." Jesus used it when he told his disciples that *all authority* in heaven and on earth had been given to him (Mt 28:18). This was the type of authority Satan tried to offer to Jesus in the wilderness. It was the authority at issue when the Jewish leaders continually questioned Jesus, "Who gave you this authority?" (Mk 11:28, 29). In every instance, this word describes an *authority*, or *power* delegated from a higher position to a lower one.

ASSUMED AUTHORITY:
KURIEUO = "TO RULE", "TO LORD OVER."

Kurieuo describes an authority that is assumed by a person on the basis of *right* or *accomplishment*. One scholar describes it as the combination of "the two elements of *power* and *authority*...the power denoted is a power of control rather than physical strength."[11] For to this end Christ died and rose and lived again, that He might *be Lord of* [have dominion over] both the dead and the living (Ro 14:9 NKJV). It could be based upon inheritance, such as the ascension of a king. It could be the result of a power struggle—victory of a military leader. Or, it could be the appointment of a local governor. For Jesus, it was the authority gained through the resurrection.

ABSOLUTE AUTHORITY:
ARCHO = "TO DOMINATE", "TO RULE", "TO BE FIRST"

"And again, Isaiah says: 'There shall be a root of Jesse; And He who shall rise *to reign* over the Gentiles, In Him the Gentiles shall hope'" (Is 11:10, Ro 15:12). *Arche*, the noun form of this word, describes one who has been elevated to the highest point. It is "primacy, whether in time or rank."[12] There can be no other above such a person. It is the same word translated *beginning*. It is used several times to proclaim Jesus as the Alpha and Omega, the Beginning and the End (Rev 1:8; 21:6; 22:19).

Not only does this word describe Jesus' authority, but Paul also used it to declare Jesus as *authority* over all *arche*.

> And you have been given fullness in Christ, who is the head over every *power* [*arche*] and *authority* [*exousia*].
> —Col 2:10

> Far above all *rule* [*arche*] and *authority* [*exousia*], *power* [*dunamis*] and *dominion* [*kuriotes*], and every title that can be given, not only in the present age but also in the one to come.
> —Eph 1:21

This is precisely what Bible writers mean when they refer to Jesus as "King of Kings and Lord of Lords" (Rev 17:14, 19:16). The point is this: "There is no one on earth, or in heaven, who has any higher authority than Jesus!" Therefore, all the word pictures used to describe Kingdom Leaders emphasize "those who are under authority" rather than "those who exercise authority."[13]

AN IMPORTANT POINT AND QUESTION

This brings us to a crucial point as we begin to make application concerning *authority* and *power* in the Kingdom. With the exception of the Apostle Paul (2Co 10:8; 13:10), these three words are not used to describe church leaders.[14] Therefore, we must ask, "What does this mean to the concept of *authority* in the local church?"

Jesus set the cornerstone of leadership within the Church and said it would be nothing like the leadership that is common throughout the world.

> But Jesus called them to *Himself* and said, "You know that the rulers of the Gentiles *lord* [*kurieuo*] it over them, and those who are great *exercise authority over* [*exousia*] them. Yet *it shall not be*

so among you; but whoever desires to become great among you, let him be your servant. And whoever desires to be first among you, let him be your slave."[15]
—Mt 20:25-27 NKJV

Let us continue past the gospels and see if there is consistency of the usage of these words. Paul said that the leadership given to him was not like the authority given him by the Chief Priest. He had experienced delegated authority (*exousia*)[16] but that was no longer important to him. In fact, Paul wrote that God would disarm and destroy all such authority.

> Then comes the end, when He delivers the kingdom to God the Father, when He puts an end to all *rule* [*arche*] and all *authority* [*exousia*] and *power* [*dunamis*]
> —1Co 15:24 NKJV

> Having disarmed *principalities* [*ache*] and *powers* [*exousia*], He made a public spectacle of them, triumphing over them in it.
> —Col 2:15 NKJV

It is important to understand that all power and authority, as recognized by the common standards of the world, are going to be destroyed. Solomon warned us to be wary of what seems right; because if it is not right with God's thinking it could end in death (Pr 16:25). The derivatives of power-based philosophies are competition and greed, which can only end in death—death for businesses, churches, families and individuals. It takes an uncommon understanding for all to grow healthy.

Since leadership does involve power and authority, where do we find a model? What is it going to look like? When we discover it, people will say, "That's not what I was taught or experienced. That is surely an uncommon concept of power and authority."

WORDS THAT DESCRIBE *FUNCTION*

God has designed my body with a pair of feet. The purpose of His design was for the feet to *function* by helping me stand or travel from one location to another. Therefore, the function of my feet is movement: however that movement might take place in different *forms*. I might walk, run, skip or jump. I might use my feet to press the accelerator of a vehicle. There are many *forms* my feet can use to fulfill their *function*.

The same is true when it comes to leadership responsibility within the church. By God's design, leadership's *function* is to meet the needs of His people. There are many *forms* in which this responsibility can be fulfilled. "God gave some to be apostles, some to be prophets, some to be evangelists, and some to be pastors and teachers." Though their form is different, their function is the same: "To prepare God's people for works of service" (Eph 4:11-12).

God is not nearly as concerned with the form we choose as He is with the function being fulfilled.

The problem arises when a person begins to think that the form he has chosen must be imposed on everyone—everyone must run; no one is allowed to walk. Or, when we look at a person who seems to be successful and determine that everyone must function according to that particular person's form.

Nowhere in the New Testament is a form of leadership clearly outlined for Kingdom Leadership structure. Some churches structure so that elders are the leaders, others push for a district bishopric as the leader, while others argue for the pastor to be first. Form will look different in various cultures and different locations. However, the function of leadership is well described. We must return our concentration to function and allow freedom in forms that fulfill it.

To understand the function of Kingdom Leadership, let us return our thinking to the uncommon paradigm of the Leader as a Shepherd. Jesus wanted to be known as *a* shepherd (Jn 10:11) and a servant (Mt 20:28). Both Paul and Peter spoke of church leaders as *shepherds* (Ac 20:28; 1Pe 5:2). The paradigm of a shepherd is that of the ultimate servant who gives his life and energy to the needs of the sheep. Nevertheless, we must recognize that shepherding is accomplished by a level of power and authority. With sheep, however, one cannot use a conventional practice of leadership—driving.

Such action causes sheep to scatter or become uncontrollable. A shepherd's authority over the sheep is gained through his or her relationship to them. Jesus explains:

> The sheep listen to his voice. He calls his own sheep by name and leads them out. When he has brought out all his own, he goes on ahead of them, and his sheep follow him because they know his voice. But they will never follow a stranger; in fact, they will run away from him because they do not recognize a stranger's voice.
> —Jn 10:3-5

It is true that shepherds serve and care for the needs of their sheep. Yet there are times when shepherds must make some hard decisions on behalf of their sheep. There are situations in which shepherds must say, "No." On other occasions the message may be, "It is time to leave this place." In the time of danger the message for the predator is, "You will not come near my sheep." At times like these, shepherds must exert their power—shepherd's power.

Kenneth Blanchard raises an important question in this context: "Are the sheep here for the shepherd, or is the shepherd here for the sheep?" He goes on to say, "The way you answer this question will determine how you lead."[17] More specifically, the answer to this question says much about the shepherd's view of power. Some leaders believe that the sheep are there for them; therefore, they use their power to get the sheep to do their bidding. The number of

Uncommon Authority

sheep in their flock is a sign of success, even power over other shepherds. Such leaders control and manipulate, demanding total obedience. They do all this while using servant language, saying they are only thinking of what is best for the sheep.

Leaders such as Moses, David, Nehemiah, Jesus, Peter, and Paul believed their function was to meet the needs of the sheep, to care for them, guide them and make them stronger. The biblical paradigm for leadership function is not authority; it is responsibility. It is not control; it is caring. It is not demanding; it is discipling. It is not preventing; it is preparing.

We have talked about the biblical words (*power* and *authority*) that are *not* used to describe Kingdom Leadership. Let us now turn our thinking to four words that describe the function of biblical leadership. It is important to remember that each definition must be measured from the Cornerstone—in light of what Jesus taught and how He functioned as a leader.

Shepherd's Power:
Poimaino = To Tend, To Lead, To Guide[18]

Four times the verb *poimaino* is used as a description of the responsibility of a leader in God's church. In each context the writer is speaking of sheep; therefore, we must translate it as *to tend, as one would tend sheep.* "The shepherd (*poimen*), as used by Jesus, is an illustration of the one who cares for sheep that belong to Jesus, the Master; it is used not as an image of authority, but as one of personal, loving care."[19]

> Again Jesus said, "Simon son of John, do you truly love me?" He answered, "Yes, Lord, you know that I love you." Jesus said, "Take care of my sheep."
> —Jn 21:16

> Keep watch over yourselves and all the flock of which the Holy Spirit has made you overseers. Be shepherds of the church of God, which he bought with his own blood.
> —Ac 20:28

> Be shepherds of God's flock that is under your care, serving as overseers—not because you must, but because you are willing, as God wants you to be; not greedy for money, but eager to serve; not lording it over those entrusted to you, but being examples to the flock. And when the Chief Shepherd appears, you will receive the crown of glory that will never fade away.
> —1Pe 5:2-4

> These men are blemishes at your love feasts, eating with you without the slightest qualm—shepherds who feed only themselves. They are clouds without rain, blown along by the wind; autumn trees, without fruit and uprooted—twice dead.
> —Jude 1:12

The paradigm of a shepherd describes the responsibility "to protect, care for, and nurture."[20]

Power is not given for the sake of control; it is given for the protection of those in the leader's care. Authority is not given for the self-preservation of the leader; it is given so that the leader can provide for others. The Shepherd paradigm is the foundation for interpreting all Scriptures concerning power and authority. They must be measured to the Good Shepherd—the Cornerstone.

Caring Authority:
Proistemi = To Stand Before

A renowned scholar on Greek language translates *proistemi*, "To stand before while caring for those being led ... the combination of leading and caring."[21] *Proistamenos* (noun) "involves the task of guarding and responsibility for and the protection of those over whom one is placed ... the verb can refer to supporting, caring and showing concern for someone.[22] It is the perfect description of a shepherd's power, of authority that flows from relationship. Jesus said that He knew the sheep by name and the sheep knew his voice and followed when He was out front leading them (Jn 10:3-5).

One example of leadership structure that has been taught for centuries[23] is called *primus inter pares*," which is translated as *first among equals*.[24] This philosophy believes that while all in the flock are equal, one has to be responsible to go first—to have the agenda and set the standards of accountability. This teaching is consistent with Paul's comments to the Corinthians where he considers himself no greater than Peter, Apollos or any other. He instructs them to "Regard us as servants of Christ" (1Co 3:5, 4:1). It agrees with Peter's statement referring to himself as a fellow-elder (1Pe 5:1).

> The one with authority is to remember that he or she is not better than the others, and the one under authority is to remember the dignity and freedom of his or her calling. Whatever may be their differences in social standing in the eyes of society, or their various responsibilities in the church, they are first and foremost partners, fellow-workers, fellow-heirs, and children of the same father.[25]

The word *proistemi* is used three times in connection with church leadership.

> …He who exhorts, in exhortation; he who gives, with liberality; *he who leads*, with diligence; he who shows mercy, with cheerfulness…
> —Ro 12:8 NKJV

> And we urge you, brethren, to recognize those who labor among you, and *are over you* in the Lord and admonish you,…
> —1Th 5:12 NKJV

> Let the elders who *rule* well be counted worthy of double honor, especially those who labor in the word and doctrine.
> —1Ti 5:17 NKJV

The New King James translation was chosen for these three verses to show how a translator using words inconsistent with the Cornerstone can cause confusion in our understanding of leadership. I have met church leaders who use 1 Timothy 5:17 as a proof text to claim their right to be "the Ruling Elder" in a congregation. However, to translate Paul's words as *ruling* is to contradict Jesus' teaching and example completely. The interpretation "to rule" is according to common thinking, not God's higher way. It does not measure from the Cornerstone. With our commitment to the sovereignty of God's Word, we must redirect our thinking accordingly. We must gently teach those who have received false instruction.

Paul uses *proistemi* to describe a Christian leader's ability to manage his home (1Ti 3:4, 5, 12; 5:17). As a measurement of one who might serve in church leadership, the Greek scholar writes, "Deacons should be heads of their households but with an emphasis on proper care for them."[26]

Proistemi describes the shepherd, or leader, standing before his flock saying, "Let's go this way." It is the picture of the shepherd who goes before his sheep always looking out for their needs and making decisions that are best for their welfare. In doing so, this leader has little care for his personal interests.

> A leader ventures to say: "I will go; come with me!" A leader initiates, provides the ideas and the structure, and takes the risk of failure along with the chance of success. A leader says: "I will go; follow me!"[27]

Sheep follow a shepherd because they have built a relationship of trust. In essence, they *give* the shepherd permission to be their leader. Power by permission is the strongest power in the world. It is also true in marriage. In Ephesians 5, wives are counseled to submit to their husband. If a husband loves according to the standard of Jesus' life and teaching, his wife would have little problem submitting to him. She would give him permission to lead (Eph 5:21-33). Children would follow their fathers (Eph 6:1-4) and slaves would follow their masters (Eph 6:5-9). When measured from the Cornerstone, all are examples of power by permission—of authority flowing from relationship.

Character Authority:
Hegeomai Or Proegeomia = To Lead, To Esteem, To Think[28]

Hebrews 13:7,17, and 24 are the verses that have probably caused the most misunderstanding in the study of Kingdom Leadership. Again, the main reason is that translators have used the common definitions of the Greek word, rather than examining the words in light of Jesus' life and teaching. God does not contradict Himself nor does He allow His Word to do so.[29]

The root word *hegeomai* describes leadership in six Scripture passages. One Greek dictionary defines *hegeomai* as *to lead, to guide, to think, to regard, or to consider*.[30] A second scholar writes, "*to esteem* is the point."[31]

Uncommon Authority

They chose Judas (called Barsabbas) and Silas, two men who were leaders (*hegeomai*) among the brothers.
—Ac 15.22

Be devoted to one another in brotherly love. Honor (*proegeomai*) one another above yourselves.
— Ro 12:10

Now we ask you, brothers, to respect those who work hard among you, who are over you (*proistemi*) in the Lord and who admonish you. Hold them in the highest regard (*hegeomai*) in love because of their work. Live in peace with each other.
—1Th 5.12-13

Remember your leaders (*hegeumenoi*), who spoke the word of God to you. Consider the outcome of their way of life and imitate their faith.
—Heb 13:7

Obey your leaders (*hegeumenoi*) and submit to their authority. They keep watch over you as men who must give an account. Obey them so that their work will be a joy, not a burden, for that would be of no advantage to you.
—Heb 13:17

Greet all your leaders (*hegeumenoi*) and all God's people.
—Heb 13:24

The consistency of our picture of a servant-leader is continued In Luke 22:26. Jesus teaches that the greatest in the Kingdom will function like the youngest, and the one who leads (*hegemonos—the one who is esteemed*) will be like one who serves (*diakonon*). Jesus' usage of *hegemonos* sets the cornerstone for the translation in Hebrews 13; therefore making translations like the King James' *rule* contradictory to Jesus' teaching.

Authority for Kingdom Leadership finds its basis in a person's character. Those who have a relationship with the leader give him permission to go in front. This permission flows from their esteem for his character and competence. As mentioned before, with the exception of managing one's household and the ability to teach, there are no leadership skills among the list of qualifications for a church leader. Christ meant for the leaders in the kingdom to be people who arrived at their position based on the esteem of their followers. He meant for leadership to flow from permission—permission granted through relationship with a leader who keeps the needs of the followers foremost.

Good Authority:
Dokeo = To Be Of Good Reputation[32]

The Greek word *dokeo* is used but once to describe church leadership. As Paul wrote the churches of Galatia, he shared his experiences with leaders in Jerusalem—those "who seemed to be leaders" (Gal 2:2). The usage of the word suggests that when

Uncommon Authority

Paul came a city or village he looked for people who were respected as leaders in the church. This word, similar to *hegeomai*, has the context of one being put into leadership because of the *esteem* of (permission given by) the people being led. People willingly followed them—not out of fear or coercion, but by choice. Sheep follow shepherds whom they trust to have their best interest at heart.

Words That Suggest *Form*

Israel looked at the surrounding secular nations and wanted their style of monarchy (leadership form). They demanded that Samuel give them a king. Samuel warned them that a king, acting like the other nations, would soon require the people to serve him (1 Sa 8:9-18). In the same way, churches have looked to the secular world and desired similar forms of leadership. During the Industrial Revolution, companies merged and formed themselves under boards that took control of the business. Churches, searching for a similar form, decided to draw ministry functions into committees, boards and/or councils to control the church's business. This form of leadership soon forgot its biblical function. Now church leaders argue over which form is correct, while function goes unheeded.

King David proved that not all kings were bad. Some, who listened to God and understood their function, were able to restore Israel and raise it above the common leadership of surrounding nations. Not all committees are bad. King or no king, leadership committee or no leadership committee, neither form is intrinsically bad. The critical question is, "What is the function of the form?" We return to the question of whether the sheep exist for shepherds or shepherds for sheep. The answer determines whether form is controlling function or function is controlling form. In most areas of the world, because of the power-based mindset of those in leadership, the function lives to protect the form—even to the point of ignoring or misinterpreting Scripture. This results in a situation similar to Ezekiel 34 where God displayed His anger against the shepherds (leaders) of Israel for failing to fulfill their function.

In order for there to be servant-based functioning of the church, the Holy Spirit chose three words to describe different forms that might perform the responsibilities God places on Kingdom Leader's. When these words are translated in agreement with the Cornerstone, they make complete sense and clarify much of the confusion about church leadership.

Servant Leader:
Diakoneo – to wait at table, to care for, to serve[33]

The verb *diakoneo* and its noun form, *diakonos*, are the most frequent words used to describe function within the body of Christ. It is also the easiest to interpret because in the Greek language there are no alternative meanings. Bromiley mentions that the use of this word went completely against the Greek philosophy of Jesus' day. "For the Greeks, service is undignified: we are born to rule, not to serve."[34] He goes on to say, "Service acquires value only when it promotes individual development of the whole."[35]

The verb *diakoneo* and the noun *diakonos* are both used to describe the ministry of angels, men, women, deacons, elders, apostles and Jesus. The verb form is translated, *wait upon someone, serve someone, care for, take care of, help,* or *support someone*.[36] Simply put, "a deacon is a servant who functions for the needs of people."

Mature Leadership:
Presbyteros = person of age, ancestors, or *elder*[37]

The most frequent word to describe a leadership form within the church is *presbyteros*. In the biblical context this word was always used to describe older, acceptably mature men within a synagogue, village or city—men of high standing in their community.[38] The use of this word would be in full agreement with *hegeomai* – "esteemed leadership." Based upon their character (1Ti 3, Tit 1) they were to direct the affairs of the church (1Ti 5:17). They were to be called to pray for the sick (Jas 5:14). They are always referred to in the plural form indicating that there was never one ruling elder. (This further affirms that the concept of a *ruling elder* does not measure to the Cornerstone.) Bennett describes the function of the *elder*.

> [The elder] is less work-oriented and more value-oriented. He gathers people and is concerned for their attitudes ... He is interested in [the church's] inner health, in the climate or environment in which the members live and which will radically alter their growth and effectiveness ...an elder seeks to maintain the body and a life-support system for believers.[39]

In every way, this describes the ministry of a shepherd creating an environment in which the sheep can be cared for and grow. It is a ministry that requires a servant's heart that thinks beyond self to the greater good of those being served.

Vigilant Leadership:
Episkeptomai, = "To look at, go to see, to visit
Episkopeo = To look upon, to care for, to oversee[40]

In English Scripture, the verb form of this word is seldom mistranslated. The Greek word is made by putting together the preposition *over* and the verb *to watch*. Thus, we get our English word *overseer*. However, only by examining the translation of the verb forms and measuring the nouns to the Cornerstone do we get a picture of the *function* of the overseer (*episkopos*).

> I was sick and you looked after (*episkeptomai*) me...
> —Mt 25:36

> Praise be to the Lord...because he has come (episkeptomai) and has redeemed his people.
> —Lk 1:68

> God has come to help (episkeptomai) his people.
> —Lk 7:16

> Religion that God our Father accepts as pure and faultless is this: to look after (episkeptomai) orphans and widows in their distress and to keep oneself from being polluted by the world.
> —Jas 1:27

Paul brings us back to the shepherd paradigm as the function of ministry. The *overseer* (elder, bishop) is one who *looks upon* the needs of people and *cares for* those needs. One Greek scholar says we must remember that "The idea of concern is present."[41] Another scholar says this verb "stresses active and responsible care."[42] This aligns with the Cornerstone and makes the meaning clear. We are not talking about a person who dominates with power and control, but rather about a person who genuinely cares about God's people and sees to their needs. We are not talking about a position with a title, but rather about active, caring ministry to the body of Christ.

> Therefore take heed to yourselves and to all the flock, among which the Holy Spirit has made you *overseers* [*episkopos*], to shepherd the church of God which He purchased with His own blood.
> —Ac 20:28 NKJV

Peter continues the shepherd metaphor and shows clearly that the function of church leadership is not to be interpreted with forms that emphasize power.

> Shepherd the flock of God which is among you, serving as *overseers (episkopeo)*, not by compulsion but willingly, not for dishonest gain but eagerly; nor as *being lords over* [*kurieuo*] those entrusted to you, but being examples to the flock.
> —1Pe 5:2-3 NKJV

Here is the problem—churches are stopped, or split, by people seeking a position of power (form), rather than desiring the honorable responsibility (1Ti 3:1) of caring for the needs of people (function). God is not overly concerned about the form leadership takes in a church or culture, or what title is given. God's concern is, "Are my sheep being cared for?"

In His teaching, Jesus emphasized a leader's obedience to God's authority rather than his exercise of authority.

> It is interesting to note that even though the disciples are being prepared for spiritual leadership in the church, Jesus places far more emphasis on their responsibility to God's authority, than on the authority which they themselves will exercise. There is far more instruction about the role of following than about the role of leading.[43]

Conclusion

In the Garden of Eden, the serpent offered power to Adam and Eve, tempting them to become as knowledgeable as God. They thought it through and did what seemed right at the time. They were wrong and were separated from God's paradise. Satan continued to offer power to prophets, priests and kings. Those who accepted his leadership imitation lost their place in God's plan. In the wilderness, Satan offered power to Jesus. However, Jesus was well acquainted with God's higher way of thinking and acting. He stayed with God's plan and became the greatest leader in world history.

Satan continues to try to lure Kingdom Leader's downward on the path of common power-based leadership philosophies. This is thinking that is based in "hollow and deceptive philosophy, which depends on human tradition and the basic principles of this world rather than on Christ" (Col 2:8). Those who hold on to God's higher way of service will be exalted in His eyes.[44] Their success will not be measured by the common standards of this world, but by those of the Chief Shepherd.

CHAPTER EIGHT

JESUS – AN INCARNATIONAL LEADER

"The Word became flesh and made his dwelling among us."
—John 1:14

"I am sorry, but you cannot use that word here." This was the concern of our translator when he heard that I was going to be teaching principles of *leadership*. In his country's history there had been a vicious dictator who had referred to himself as "The Leader," thus the word brought painful memories. After an hour of discussing alternatives we settled on a word that means, "man in the front." Once during the session the translator slipped and used the *forbidden* word and the entire audience gasped. It became very obvious to me how much misery this *leader* had caused his people.

In other cultures people have difficulty with the word *servant*. There are individuals who rebel at the thought of serving; however, I am speaking of cultures where the word has other usage. In one southern African culture the word *servant* refers to a person who is attached to a spirit and does its bidding. Other cultures cannot separate the concept of *servant* from *slavery*. Therefore, we must be careful in our selection of words until we can develop the biblical concept of the *caretaker*.

When Jesus tried to help his disciples understand *servanthood* he used words that created pictures in their minds to explain the concept. One of those pictures was "The Good Shepherd." As seen in our discussion in chapter 5, Jesus was not talking about an absentee owner of the sheep who hires someone else to care for his sheep. Jesus described an owner who lives among the sheep and knows their names and needs. This owner is willing to risk his life to protect and provide for his flock. The Incarnate Jesus is the owner who came to live among His sheep. He was the fulfillment of Isaiah's prophecy declaring that the Messiah would be *Emmanuel*, "God with us" (Isa 7:14).

Plato developed much of his philosophy by studying the actions of the gods of Greek mythology who seldom ever left their places on Mount Olympus. They were too busy with parties and fighting among themselves to be concerned about *mortals*. Therefore, they sent messengers to do their bidding and to deliver their mandates.

Jesus – An Incarnational Leader

Arising from Plato's concepts, modern leadership understands success as climbing higher in the leadership structure to the point that servants are available to do one's bidding. Such leaders function behind closed doors, are protected by those who serve them, and seldom meet anyone beyond their staffs. They do not know names or needs. They are isolated rulers.

The Apostle John makes a bold statement in the beginning of his gospel record by declaring that God's Word became flesh and lived among us (Jn 1:14). The literal translation is, "He pitched His tent in our midst." Jesus entered into a world of isolated leadership and through teaching and action presented an uncommon concept of how leaders relate to their people.

The fact that Jesus, the owner of the sheep, came to experience life among the sheep is known in theology as *The Incarnation*, or, *in the flesh*. This uncommon concept of leadership speaks strongly to what is expected of a Kingdom Leader and sets another mark on the Cornerstone from which we measure. Let us examine the leadership example of Jesus as an *Incarnational Leader*—one who comes among the people and fulfills our definition of leadership.

One of the strongest leadership lessons Jesus taught is recorded in John 13. The key to understanding the impact of this lesson is found in verse three, where John writes, "Jesus knew that the Father had put all things under His power." Later Jesus tells His disciples, "You call me teacher and Lord, and rightly so" (Jn 13:13). John wants us to know that Jesus knew who He was; that He knew he already possessed full authority and power. However, as the disciples struggled to determine which one of them was the most important, Jesus took a towel and basin, assuming the responsibilities of the lowest slave in the house. Such an act was so uncommon in their experience that the disciples were nearly speechless as Jesus knelt before them. Jesus told them, "This is the type of leadership I expect from you" (Jn 13:15). Jesus taught it as the Shepherd's Paradigm. Now he models it as the Cornerstone from which all leadership is measured.

Incarnational leadership is as uncommon in our modern power-based world as it was in biblical times. However, no other leadership style better describes His actions. Working in relationship with one's people fits the definition we have measured from The Cornerstone.

Incarnational Leadership Builds Relationships

The narrative of what happened in the Upper Room begins with a strong statement of relationship. "Having loved his own who were in the world, he now showed them the full extent of his love" (Jn 13:1). Jesus had carefully chosen and trained the people gathered in the room that night before he died. He had walked with them for three years and knew them intimately. His leadership grew out of this relationship.

The disciples were not the only people with whom Jesus built an incarnational relationship.

> Jesus went through all the towns and villages, teaching in their synagogues, preaching the good news of the kingdom and healing every disease and sickness. When He saw the crowds He had compassion on them, because they were like sheep without a shepherd.
> —Mt 9:35-36

This is a powerful statement concerning His incarnational leadership. The impact that Jesus made was not simply because of His title of "Son of God" or the quality of His teaching. Jesus did not follow the common practice of his day, which was to establish Himself in a major city and draw students to come sit at His feet. He walked among the common people with an uncommon presence. His teaching was directed at their needs, communicated in word pictures they could understand. He was not unaware of their daily struggles and showed a genuine concern for His audience. While Jewish leaders studied for reasons to isolate themselves from women, children, the poor, the sick and the lame, Jesus ate with sinners, touched lepers, welcomed children and ministered to the poor. In a culture where leadership commonly ignored people of lower status, Jesus, as the incarnation of deity, showed an uncommon compassion for all and purposely built relationships with them.

INCARNATIONAL LEADERSHIP IS SERVICE

Jesus set the cornerstone for servant leadership in a way that could only be done by an incarnational leader. He got up from the meal and took off his outer garment (Jn 13:4). In Jewish leadership culture the outer garment was the sign of his office. Pharisees and Sadducees spent great amounts of money on their clothes to display their wealth and importance.[1] Jesus, the Son of God (who did not count equality with God as important as serving people's needs), emptied himself and took on the form of a servant (Php 2:5-6).

After stripping Himself of His cloak, Jesus performed the duties of the lowest household slave.[2] While the disciples argued over who was the most important (Lk 22:24), Jesus took a towel and a basin of water and began to wash their feet. Someone should have been there to do this service when the disciples arrived. None, however, had volunteered to bow before their colleagues to refresh them from their dusty travels.

After washing their feet, Jesus instructed them not to think like the non-Kingdom Leader's they knew. Those leaders loved to "lord it over" their people. Jesus very clearly said, "It will not be so with you" (Mk 10:42). He told them that titles such as "Lord and Teacher" were not the basis of leadership responsibility. He, their Lord and Teacher, had taken on the role of the lowest servant, and they were no greater than He. Therefore, they must be willing to do the same (Jn 13:13-17). Incarnational leadership only performs in the realm of *service*. As Edersheim writes, " service [is] the evidence of rule."[3]

INCARNATIONAL LEADERSHIP IS DEDICATED

The common thinking of the world seeks for opportunities to climb higher in the leadership structure. Everything is evaluated by how it will help one on the path to his success. A person is considered *dedicated* by forfeiting family and friends. The aspiring leader is required to work long hours to prove dedication and gain promotions. In our western culture it is referred to as being *married* to the company,

When Jesus entered the upper room with His disciples His thoughts focused on, "How can I prepare these men to be effective? How can I teach them?" In His dedication to helping His followers see the true picture of servant-leadership, He gave an incarnational demonstration.

Throughout His ministry we see Jesus' compassion for people in all strata of life. We recognize his confident authority as he taught and dealt with their problems. We watch as He confronts those who use people rather than help them. We read of his commitment to training those who would fulfill

His Father's vision. We stand in awe of His complete sacrifice for people.

When I was a student in high school, I once sought some help from a teacher after his class was over. He walked out the door and said, "I cannot help you." Jokingly I asked him, "What about all this dedication of teachers I hear about?" He turned to me and said, "Mine ends the minute the clock says, 'class is over.'" Yet, Jesus was willing to be disturbed by children wanting to be held, by hurting people crying out from the roadside, by people summoning him to come to the aid of an ill friend or relative. Jesus' dedication to His Father's purpose did not stop when it was no longer convenient for Him.

Perhaps one of the strongest statements of Jesus' dedication to serving the deepest needs of people is found in Luke's words, "As the time approached for him to be taken up to heaven, Jesus resolutely set out for Jerusalem" (Lk 9:51). Nothing was going to stop Jesus as He headed to the cross. There was no personal concern or self-promotion in His steps. There was no running to isolation. This was an act of courage and selflessness. Jesus was dedicated to being among His people until the end.

INCARNATIONAL LEADERSHIP ASSISTS

After Jesus had washed the disciple's feet He asked, "Do you understand what I have done?" (Jn 13:12). So many times during His ministry Jesus had taken special time with His followers to explain a teaching, to give further instruction, or to help them understand why they were not able to perform a miracle. The very essence of being a servant is to *assist* people.

As I write this chapter there is a very popular American TV show that has made common the phrase, "You're fired!" The show begins with one of America's most well-known businessmen choosing eighteen people and giving them an opportunity to demonstrate why he should hire them. Each week he assigns the apprentices a task and then he retreats to his office. At the end of the week they are brought before him to report and one is fired. Never once in the weeks of this program does this man give any assistance to the apprentices, only criticism and dismissal. He continually asks them, "Who is the weakest? Who would you fire?" By my observation the main lessons these twelve candidates have learned is how to manipulate the system and how to make the others look bad. They are learning to promote themselves, not assist each other's success. They have learned to follow Machiavelli's advice: "Do all you can to weaken those who are more powerful."[4]

Jesus fought against this type of thinking with his apprentices. He wanted each of them to succeed in their Kingdom tasks. He would not allow conversations about who was the greatest.

Perhaps a similar example to the American TV show was when Jesus sent twelve disciples to preach. Mark and Luke record the event. However, in contrast to the American businessman, Jesus spent at least two years teaching these men before He assigned the task. He gave them specific instructions (Mk 6:7-11; Lk 9:1-6). They were sent out to preach in the surrounding villages and minister to the needs of people. When they returned, there was no harsh criticism, no questions about who was best. No one was fired. Instead, Jesus took them to a quiet place where they could rest and share what they had learned (Mk 6:30-31; Lk 9:10).

Jesus' willingness to be present to assist His followers in fulfilling their ministry did not end with His presence on earth. He promised to be with them as long as this world continued to exist (Mt 28:20). He promised to send them another Assistant (Jn 14:16) to help them in their Kingdom work. The incarnational existence of the presence of God was going to continue.

INCARNATIONAL LEADERSHIP LIFTS OTHERS TO POTENTIAL

According to Luke, following the Last Supper the disciples once again began to argue over who was the most important in the new Kingdom (22:26). Perhaps it was at this time that Jesus began washing their feet. Jesus stopped the Upper Room argument by declaring, "The one who serves is greater than the one served." (Lk 22:27) This statement is in complete contrast to the common principles of Greek philosophy that controlled thinking then and now.

When Jesus had completed His service of washing the disciples' feet, He told them, "You will be blessed if you do this" (Jn 13:17). The word Jesus used for *blessed* should not be understood in the common sense of "if you do this, you will receive personal gain." This is the same word Jesus used in the Beatitudes (Mt 5:1-12).[5] It means, "you will have *joy*, be *fulfilled*, if you serve as I have served." His definition of success focused on leaders helping meet the needs of those in their care.

One of the strongest examples of Jesus' incarnational leadership and dedication to His disciples' success took place on the shores of Galilee after his resurrection. Peter believed he was a failure and undesirable in the eyes of Jesus. He had betrayed Him rather than dying for Him. Jesus came to Peter to restore him to ministry (Jn 21:15-23). Perhaps, even as Jesus had spoken to His disciples in the Upper Room, we can hear Jesus say to us following His encounter with Peter, "I have set an example for you, do as I have done" (Jn 13:15).

THE IMPACT OF INCARNATIONAL LEADERSHIP

While I was in seminary, our professor assigned each student a word from the Greek New Testament. We were to prepare an oral presentation that explained how it was used in the context of ministry. One student, a linguistics major, was assigned the word *logos*, which the Apostle John used to describe Jesus in the opening of his gospel. In his report to the class, the student claimed that a possible translation of *logos* would be *impact*.

This word *logos*, which John chose to describe Jesus, is not the common word for *word*. The more frequent usage is *rhema,* which indicates an announcement.[6] However, John uses the less common word, *logos*, which is used when the speaker expects a response. Because *logos* demands a response, *impact* was suggested as a possible translation.[7]

Because *logos* demands response by the hearer, the Apostle John was saying that Jesus came from God to impact the world. He made this impact by leaving heaven to come into our midst [*incarnation*] to share the redemption message and model God's desires (Php 2:5-11). Now we must respond.

> The Incarnation of Jesus Christ is the pivot upon which our world turns. Whether to understand His life or His leadership; we must begin with the Incarnation. Then, from the mystery of its paradox and the miracle of its resolution, the meaning of the *Word became flesh* unfolds before us. From His Incarnate character we learn the meaning of His redemptive vision, His servant strategy and His teaching task. Likewise, by experiencing the Incarnation for ourselves, we learn that Christian leaders are different in *being* as well as *doing*. Our incarnational *being* is *to embody the Spirit of Christ*; our incarnational *doing* is *to empower His people.*[8]

> Secular leadership theory tends to emphasize the organization and the process more than the person...Christian leadership is different because it

centers in the character of the person and engages spiritual as well as human resources.[9]

As Jesus impacts the life of a Kingdom Leader He demands a response that effects the leader's being. The leader, like the incarnate Christ, is no longer self-centered, but other-centered. Thus, not only is the leader's character changed, but also his priorities and actions. Common leadership philosophy has little to say about the character of a leader. It is more concerned with a leader's personality *traits* that can, as in the Greek concept of *logos*, control.

Jesus impacted an entire world with twelve men whom few people saw as leaders. They were a mixture of common men who did not have the *traits* their world considered necessary for leadership. Their personalities and skills were varied. He changed them by living among them and modeling a new concept of leadership. He did it by serving rather than commanding.

"The Word became flesh and dwelt among us." It was that dwelling that impacted us so greatly. His were not just important words spoken from heaven, but words lived out among people. McKenna claims that Jesus was much "more of a coach than a commander."[10] He was willing to go among his people and know their needs first hand. He was willing to get to know life as his people lived it. He was willing to experience the rigors of the labor force—carpenter, fisherman and rabbi. He was willing to meet people's needs. He was willing to train others to do what he did. He was willing to take risks that involved people. He was willing to forgive when people failed.

Jesus is the supreme model of leadership. He is the shepherd that stands in front saying, "Follow me." No other historical leader has accomplished as much as He in such a short period of time. His life and teaching are still impacting every nation of the earth. He is the model of leadership character by embodying active caring. He is the model of leadership action by assisting others to grow.

How did Jesus, The Word, impact the world? He created it, sustains it, entered it and saved it. He did not count a hallowed position in heaven as being important. He left it and entered into our life. He came to bring a message and a model into the midst of people who needed to know it. Now, we must again hear His words, "I have set you an example that you should do as I have done for you" (Jn 13:15).

CHAPTER NINE

DAVID – RULER IN RIGHTEOUSNESS

"The LORD rewards every man for his righteousness and faithfulness."
—1 Samuel 26:23

Having seen the incarnational example of Jesus, and in light of what we have discovered about God's emphasis on the heart of a leader, it would be good for us to look at the lives of two leaders who became examples of the uncommon leadership God desires. In this chapter we will look at the heart of King David, a ruler in God's earthly Kingdom—Israel. In the next chapter we will examine the ministry of the Apostle Paul.

It would be hard to deny that David was the greatest ruler to sit on Israel's throne as he took Israel into its "Golden Age." God testified that

David was "a man after my own heart" (Ac 13:22). Asaph, writer of many of Israel's songs, reported that David "shepherded Israel with integrity of heart" (Ps 78:72).

When David's life was ebbing away, he spoke an oracle to all who would follow him on the throne. An oracle is a pronouncement from God concerning the future. Therefore, David's words are as important to Kingdom Leaders today as they were to his sons who followed in his lineage.

> The Spirit of the LORD spoke through me; his word was on my tongue. The God of Israel spoke, the Rock of Israel said to me: 'When one rules over men in righteousness, when he rules in the fear of God, he is like the light of morning at sunrise on a cloudless morning, like the brightness after rain that brings the grass from the earth.
> —2 Sa 23:2-4

For the next 230 years following David's death, twenty-six men sat on the thrones of Israel and Judah, and most of them traced their lineage back to David. Only nine would "do right in the eyes of the Lord." Only five of these nine would take a stand against idolatry and lead Israel in "righteousness." In fact, David's own son, Solomon, turned his heart away from God to follow after idols introduced by his many wives (1Ki 11:9). This began God's displeasure with the Kingdom Leaders who failed to heed this oracle given through David. However, when Kingdom Leaders like Josiah had hearts that were responsive to God, they received His blessing (1Ki 22:19).

In this chapter I want to examine David's last words and set them as an example to all Kingdom Leaders. I believe this oracle which God gave through David provides both a challenge and a promise.

THE CHALLENGE

—2 Samuel 23:3

To Live Righteously

Before we can "rule in righteousness" we have to be living a life of righteousness. The Hebrew word David chose for his admonition means, "to be right in conduct and character." Before we can teach or preach righteousness we must be able to model it. Before we can demand it in others we must be demanding it in ourselves. Perhaps this is why the qualifications for New Testament leadership deal mainly with character issues (1Ti 3; Tit 1).

When we speak of righteousness in connection with David the first question that comes to mind is, "What about Bathsheba?" How could David claim, "I am not guilty of wrongdoing or rebellions" (1Sa 24:11) in light of his sinful affair and its murderous cover-up? How did David become such a successful leader, who could then announce, "The Lord dealt with me according to my righteousness?"(2Sa 22:21, 25). The answer is in David's acknowledgement and response to his sin. He never denied the sin. He did not attempt to redefine sin to allow for his actions. He realized that the first "person" he let down was God, who had called him to lead Israel. When he admitted his sin, the prophet told him he had been forgiven (2Sa 12:13). When God pronounces us clean, we should not again refer to ourselves as dirty.

David prayed, "Judge me according to my righteousness, according to my integrity" (Ps 7:8-9). Integrity has been defined as "what we are when no one is watching". It is a consistency of belief and action wherever we are, whomever we are with. Once I was speaking to a local businessman about an elder in the church where I served. When the businessman realized whom I was referring to, he told me, "If that man is an elder in your church, I don't want anything to do with it." He went on to talk about the man's language and laziness.

On another occasion a certain man was nominated to become an elder in our congregation. We asked the congregation if they knew any reason why this man should not be an elder. One person reported how the potential elder had bragged about cheating a pastor in a business deal. People in his Bible study told how he claimed that he had not paid his taxes for seven years. There was no way we could allow this man to become a spiritual leader of our congregation.

Neither of these church leaders was living a life of integrity. They were not qualified to "lead in righteousness" because righteousness was not present in their own lives.

David knew that the temptation to breach integrity is strong for those in leadership, especially when one is convinced that no one is going to know. The king had fallen and suffered the stinging discipline of God for his sin with Bathsheba. We read of his sorrow and repentance in Psalms 32 and 51. Perhaps this is why David added, "When he rules in the fear of God."

In Psalm 36 David claimed that integrity is lost as a person convinces himself or herself that God will not know. He attributes it to the fact that there is "no fear of God." Righteousness is broken because desire becomes stronger than fear. Desire thus causes a person to say, "I don't think God knows or cares if I commit this act. " Here are David's words:

> An oracle is within my heart concerning the sinfulness of the wicked: There is no fear of God before his eyes. For in his own eyes he flatters himself too much to detect or hate his sin. The words of his mouth are wicked and deceitful; he has ceased to be wise and to do good. Even on his bed he plots evil; he commits himself to a sinful course and does not reject what is wrong.
> —Ps 36:1-4

David believed that only a righteous person could "dwell on God's holy hill". He describes righteousness by giving us a definition of integrity.

> He whose walk is blameless and who does what is righteous, who speaks the truth from his heart and has no slander on his tongue, who does his neighbor no wrong and casts no slur on his fellowman, who despises a vile man but honors those who fear the Lord, who keeps his oath even when it hurts, who lends his money without usury and does not accept a bribe against the innocent. He who does these things will never be shaken.
> —Ps 15:1-5

Not only did David strive to live a holy life, he held his men accountable for their actions. When he went to Ahimelech to ask for bread for his men, the priest asked him if his men were clean. David replied, "Indeed women have been kept from us, as usual whenever I set out. The men's things are holy even on missions that are not holy" (1Sa 21:5). Later, while he was still running from Saul, David had his men protect women who were in the midst of sheep shearing. One of the servants reported, "These men were very good to us. They did not mistreat us, and the whole time we were out in the fields near them nothing was missing" (1Sa 25:15).

While people pretend to judge one another according to outward appearances, God is examining the heart (1Sa 16:7). He knows the purpose of every action. He even knows the secrets of our heart, secrets we believe we have hidden (1Ki 8:39; Ps 44:21). David believed that God was not above putting people in situations that test their hearts to display their integrity (1Ch 29:17).

David – Ruler in Righteousness

Whenever God gives a list of leadership qualifications, that list emphasizes the character—the righteousness—of the one being called. Therefore David's oracle is more than just final words; it is a summation of what God is looking for in leadership.

A leader who truly fears God will display a true heart, no matter the place, the circumstances, or the audience. To get there, David had looked to God as his Ruler (Ps 5:8). To receive the promises of this oracle, a leader must lead in righteousness—making sure his or her relationship with God is right.

Treat People Righteously

A second part of "ruling in righteousness" is not only to live morally right, but also to do what is right for people. The Hebrew word David chose for rule means, "to have dominion over." We cannot talk about leadership without coming to the question of power. Power is a reality; it is a part of leadership. Again, as I mentioned in chapter seven, the question is what are we going to do with power, authority, position or title—control people or build people? There is negative power and there is positive power. One puts the emphasis on the desires of the ruler; the latter puts the emphasis on the needs of those being ruled. David is calling future generations of Kingdom Leaders to rule with positive power.

Let's refresh our thinking on two important questions. "Are the sheep there for the shepherd, or is the shepherd there for the sheep?" "Did God create the garden for His children or His children for the garden?" The answers will determine our use of power. When David became king, the people reminded him of God's words and how He put shepherding and ruling together. "The LORD said to you, 'You will shepherd my people Israel, and you will become their ruler'" (2Sa 5:2). The psalmist Asaph testifies that David lived up to these words as he "shepherded with integrity" (Ps 78:72).

Perhaps a review of the Greek word that is chosen to translate the Hebrew concept of rule will help our understanding. As we saw in chapter 8, the word, found in Hebrews 13:7 and 17, is literally translated, "To lead with care." Our understanding of this concept of rule makes a tremendous difference in how we see people. The second most common word used to describe Kingdom Leadership means, "a combination of leading and caring." When we measure the concept of rule back to the Cornerstone, it is safe to say that we are not put in control over people, but rather we are given responsibility to care for people.

All through David's life we see glimpses of his leadership and righteous treatment of his people. Probably one of the best illustrations is found in 1 Samuel 30. David and his men were fleeing from Saul, enduring heavy physical and psychological pressure. After a year of faithful service to Achish they were sent home, unwanted. When they arrived home, their village had been burned; their women and children were taken captive. David and his soldiers set out to bring their families back. However, David did not move without inquiring of the Lord. David understood his men's anguish and did not retaliate when they turned against him. As they tracked their enemy, David did not push them beyond their endurance. When the victory was won and the spoils were being recovered, David not only divided them equally with all his men, but also with the cities that helped.

To rule in righteousness is to lead people in the same spirit in which God rules His people. This is why the New Testament word emphasizes "care" (which is consistent with love and grace). This is why in both Old and New Testaments leaders are referred to as "shepherds." If we want to understand God's leadership heart, we must turn to Psalm 23 where the Lord/Shepherd provided, led, restored, and protected His sheep. Or perhaps turn to John 13:4-5, to Jesus' example as " ... he got up from the meal, took off his outer clothing, and wrapped a towel around his waist ... and began to wash his disciples' feet." He did this knowing "that the Father had put all things under his power." Being all-powerful did not mean having all serve Him.

Only one generation removed from David's righteous rule, a decision was made that affected the rest of Israel's history. This decision was based squarely on the question of care or control. David's grandson, Rehoboam, wanted to know the best way for him to rule. His choice was between the way his grandfather had ruled (with a heart for God and His people), or to rule in the same manner as neighboring kings (with a strong hand over God's people). He called in his father's advisors and they counseled, "serve the people and they will always be with you" (1Ki 12:7). In other words, "rule in righteousness."

Rehoboam was not pleased with this response, so he called in younger advisors who were more sensitive to his desires. They told him to lay on a "heavy yoke", i.e. "show them who is boss" (1Ki 12:10). Rehoboam ignored the first advisers; in heeding the second group, he chose power. The result was the dividing of the kingdom and the loss of God's blessing.

Any time we choose power over service, we stand to lose everything we would hope to gain, for now and eternity. Nineteen of the kings that followed David's oracle chose power for their leadership tool. Their stories are full of evil, corruption, murder and misery for leader and people. David became a servant to his people. The results are best reported following his period of mourning for his general, Abner. "All the people took note and were pleased; indeed, everything the king did pleased them" (2Sa 3:36).

As we accept the mantle of Kingdom Leadership we also face "Rehoboam's Choice." Will we choose power or righteousness? If we make the right choice, the promises of David's oracle will be ours. Therefore, let us examine those promises.

The Promises: "You Will Be Like…"
—2 Samuel 23:14

1. "Sunrise on a cloudless morning."

This is a beautiful picture of joy and freshness. I know few people who do not enjoy a bright sunny morning where life springs to action. In contrast, we know what it is like getting up on a cold, damp, gray morning. We just want to roll over and sleep some more. Grey is depressing. However, bright sunshine welcomes us and refreshes our spirits.

Under a power-based ruler like Rehoboam, people may dread coming together and begin to look for reasons to stay home. Perhaps some will persevere, but only because duty or habit draws them. Their spirits are gray and depressed. They are going through spiritual motions with little or no blessing. Power-based leadership will produce an atmosphere of fear and anger, rather than joy and hope.

Under a righteous ruler like David, people are glad to come to the house of the Lord. David said, "I was glad when they said, 'Let's go into the house of the Lord'" (Ps 122:1). There is joy, fellowship, peace and freedom. Only during the periods of righteous kings did Judah experience this freshness within their soul.

2. "Rain that brings green growth."

We rejoice at an afternoon's rain that nourishes our fields. We also rejoice in the bright beauty of clean sunshine after the rain. The combination of the two brings "green growth."

In the study of leadership principles we discover that power-based leaders, such as Rehoboam, cannot afford to allow people to grow, lest they become more powerful than their leaders. Followers must be kept ignorant and under control, or so the thinking goes. But this only quenches the Spirit of God and the joy of the people.

Leadership teacher, Henri Nouwen, questions how Christian leaders, in the light of Jesus' example and teaching, find it so easy to give in to the temptation for power, and, to do so in the name of a Savior and Leader who emptied himself of power

In contrast, studies show that righteous leaders, such as David, promote growth in people's relationship with God and each other. As light reveals truth, the decisions of a righteous leader will never make God's people compromise their relationship with The Almighty. As light shows the way, the teachings of a righteous leader will be a light to lead their followers in discovering God's will. As light brings healing, so the righteous leader's godly counsel will bring healing to troubles.

Conclusion

There we have them, David's final words spoken to future generations of leaders. They confront us when we find ourselves faced with Rehoboam's Choice—service or power? Will we listen to the wisdom of one of God's finest, or will we listen to the wisdom of the world and do what is common? Nowhere in David's life and teaching was there ever an emphasis on power or position. He was a servant of God and His people. As such, he becomes our first example. However, the same can be said of all other righteous Old Testament leaders. Abraham, Moses, Joshua, Samuel, and Nehemiah also focused on their personal relationship with God and the needs of His people.

As we close this chapter on David's leadership, let us note that in Psalm 5:12 he adds a third promise for the righteous ruler—He "will be blessed by God." What further affirmation does a leader need? What more can we desire?

CHAPTER TEN

PAUL – BUILDER OF PEOPLE

"My purpose is that they may be encouraged in heart and united in love."
—Colossians 2:2

I once worked with an associate pastor who loved to have opportunities to preach. However, every time he delivered a sermon people would ask, "Why is he so angry?" This man saw preaching as an opportunity to scold and criticize the people. Soon, when people heard that he was going to preach, they stayed home because they felt so torn down and defeated by his words. This man's approach to preaching is not unusual around the world. Such leaders see their responsibility as announcing what is wrong with society and with hearers.

As we continue our study of Kingdom Leaders who have God's heart, we turn from King David to the Apostle Paul. We are privileged to see the two halves of this man's life. We first see him as Saul of Tarsus, a zealous leader boldly dedicated to doing everything within his power to oppose the name of Jesus (Ac 26:9). With authority from the chief priests, he put Christians in prison and voted for their execution (Ac 9:14). He went from one synagogue to another to force believers to deny Jesus. If they would not, he punished them. He described his actions as an obsession (Ac 26:10-11).

A more familiar picture of this man is the one following his conversion and subsequent name change to Paul. The zeal for serving God was still present, but his focus and purpose were totally changed. No longer was he the power driven leader we met before Damascus. His new desire was to build up (strengthen) those who believe in Jesus (1Co 13:10).

My heart breaks today when I see Kingdom Leaders so focused on the world's definitions and examples. The world emphasizes the external—strength, numbers, titles and wealth. Paul was familiar with this mindset himself. He was steeped in the Greek philosophy that taught power and control by the strongest. He knew the teachings that had corrupted James and John into thinking they had to have important positions in the new kingdom Jesus was establishing (Mk 10:37). Paul stood against those who held to this secular philosophy of leadership. He referred to them as those who "take pride in what is seen" and contrasted them to leaders who have the heart of God (2Co 5:12).

Paul had gone from a leader who had caused suffering within Christ's Body to one who gladly suffered on its behalf (Col 1:24). He says he had been commissioned as a *servant* of the church to build up the church. This transition from a power hungry leader to a servant is a very important study for those seeking to understand what God desires from those He calls to leadership. Therefore, let's take a closer look at the Apostle and learn from both his new message and his new method of leadership.

Paul's Message of Building People

Paul wrote that it was his desire to serve God with his whole heart by preaching the good news brought by Jesus (Ro 1:9). The message of Christ's death, burial and resurrection was the most important part of his ministry (1Co 15:3-4). He knew that all the power a person needed was resident in this message that could bring salvation to souls estranged from God (Ro 1:16).

Paul's description of the message he was given to preach challenges all who have been called to Kingdom Leadership. He had learned it from Jesus as he was instructed in Arabia (Gal 1:17-18). The Lord gave him the message of grace that Jesus himself had introduced in place of the Law (Jn 1:15-16). When Saul of Tarsus marched to Damascus, he did so with the authority of the Law to bind people (Ac 9:14). Now Paul marched across the map with a new authority—God's commission to serve by preaching a message of grace that builds people (2Co 10:13). His was a message and service of uncommon love.

Fourteen times Paul uses the Greek word *oikodomeo* (to build up, to strengthen, to edify) to describe ministry. The Lord confirmed in Paul a message of grace that builds (Eph 4:29—"benefits" NIV), and he, in turn, passed the message to all Kingdom Leaders. He told the Ephesian elders that their responsibility was "the word of grace, which can build up" (Ac 20:32). To the Corinthians he wrote:

> For we are God's fellow workers; you are God's field, God's building. By the grace God has given me, I laid a foundation as an expert builder, and someone else is building on it. But each one should be careful how he builds. For no one can lay any foundation other than the one already laid, which is Jesus Christ.
>
> —1Co 3:9-11

Paul's message to Kingdom Leaders in Rome, Corinth and Ephesus are consistent. Those who have been called to preach, teach, or lead in other ways in the Kingdom must see their work as a building ministry. However, Paul is not talking about ministries to simply build large buildings or attract large crowds. He said we must be careful not to judge success by outward appearances, but by what is happening in the leader's heart and in the hearts of the people (2Co 5:12).

In his first letter to Corinth Paul warned, "Knowledge puffs up, but love builds up" (1Co

8.1). Later he guided them to "...excel in gifts that build up the church" (1Co 14:12). Again, he was not talking about numbers, but rather about building people so they are stronger in faith and more capable of fulfilling their ministry within the Kingdom. He told the Roman Christians, "Let us therefore make every effort to do what leads to peace and to mutual edification (*oikodomeo*—building up, strengthening) (Ro 14:19). He directed the Thessalonians to "encourage one another and build each other up" (1Th 5.11).

Leaders must constantly search their hearts to discern their motives for leading. The motive for some is to rebuke and correct, saying such things as, "I'm going to wake these people up, straighten them out and get them to live like they should." Others lead for the satisfaction of getting people to follow. Another might say, "I worked hard on this message and these people are going to hear it." A Kingdom Leader, however, is always asking, "What can I do to make people stronger?" The focus is on building people up, not tearing them down.

A pastor once responded to this teaching by saying, "Sometimes you have to tear down the old before you can build the new." That may be true. We can certainly find occasions when Paul used words like *confront, rebuke, admonish* and *warn*. However, in Paul's context are these actions not loving responses of a shepherd, rather than the heavy hand of a ruler?

Consider how long it takes to tear down a house, compared to the time it takes to build one. Given that example, then should we not spend more time building up rather than in tearing down? Compare the number of Scriptures where Paul uses the negative words to the number of times he uses words like *build up, strengthen, encourage, grow* and *mature*.[1]

Paul's ministry was focused on building believers who were prepared to do works of service within the Kingdom (Eph 4:12-13). He labored to present everyone perfect (mature) in Christ (Col 1:28). He knew this goal would be accomplished when believers were encouraged and united in love (Col 2:2).

> … liberating people to do what is required of them in the most effective and humane way possible. Thus the leader is the servant of his followers in that he removes the obstacles that prevent them from doing their jobs. In short, the true leader enables his or her followers to realize their full potential.[2]

By reading through Paul's letters we begin to pick up many of his thoughts on "how to build people." For instance, in 1 Corinthians 8:1 and Ephesians 4:16 he tells his readers that it is love that builds people. He also tells Christians to be careful of what comes out of their mouths. We are to make sure it is "only what is helpful for building others up" (Eph 4:29). And, just what is it that builds people up?

> Whatever is true, whatever is noble, whatever is right, whatever is pure, whatever is lovely,

whatever is admirable—if anything is excellent or praiseworthy—think about such things.
—Php 4:8

Encouragement builds people up (1Th 5:11) as does looking for ways to "spur one another on toward love and good deeds" (Heb 10:24). All of us as leaders are to do our job in such a way that prepares God's people "for works of service, so that the body of Christ may be built up" (Eph 4:12).

These lessons we learn from Paul are a real threat to power-based leaders. When leaders believe that success is found in controlling and ruling, they cannot allow people to grow, lest the followers gain more power than the leader. Persons addicted to power become accustomed to having people look to them for needs and direction. A growing person might discover inner resources that lessen such dependence. Keeping people ignorant and discouraged is the best way to keep them dependent. Therefore a power-based leader will purposely withhold information that could strengthen people and continually remind their followers of their weaknesses and unworthiness, thereby denying people opportunities for growth.

As I teach in the university and in various countries, I continually hear of churches and businesses that failed because there was no leader available when God removed the power-based person. Training, knowledge and/or experience that would have produced a second-generation leader were withheld for fear of losing position, power or title. One of two results will take place when there is no provision for training second generation leaders: the church or business will die, or a new leader will rise up to take the mantle of power. Leadership based on power will always feel threatened by the growth of another person. Leadership based on service will always rejoice in the growth of others.

Allow me to repeat a quote from chapter one:

> "A servant-leader *is* a servant first...[A leader's responsibility is] To make sure other people's highest priority needs are being served. The best test, and difficult to administer, is do those served grow as persons? Do they, *while being served*, become healthier, wiser, freer, more autonomous, more likely themselves to become servants?"[3]

One test of true leadership, therefore, is to look back on those you have been leading. Have these people been growing stronger in their relationship with the Lord? Are they more capable today to do works of service than they were when you first became their leader? How many Kingdom Leaders have been prepared and launched into leadership as a result of your leadership?

PAUL'S EXAMPLE AS A PEOPLE BUILDER

Paul saw the people in God's Kingdom as if they were family and treated them with the love and respect due to family members. Kingdom Leaders will find this to be the most effective guideline for strengthening and building people.

In most of the world's cultures, family is the most important of all relationships. Greater than the emotional ties that exist in families is the feeling of deep respect for each person's position in that family. This is difficult for people in western cultures to understand because we so strongly value individualism. However, in most other cultures, it is the family that is most important, not the individual. To properly understand how Paul saw his leadership after his conversion, we must return our thinking to the strong sense of family (as opposed to *individualism*) found in other cultures.

Writing to the young evangelist, Timothy, Paul told him the best way to approach people so that he can be trusted as their leader.

> Do not rebuke an older man harshly, but exhort him as if he were your father. Treat younger men as brothers, older women as mothers, and younger women as sisters, with absolute purity.
> —1Ti 5:1,2

These are not idle words spoken by the apostle. This is exactly the kind of respect expected of a Kingdom Leader. In many cultures one would never speak disrespectfully to an elder. The same guideline stands in the Kingdom. To treat an older woman as if she were your mother gives us a new picture of leadership responsibility that is far from the controlling power displays that are common, especially in the western world. One hundred twenty-eight times in his letters, Paul chose the word *brother* to describe his relationship with young men and other church leaders. When he used the word *sister* to describe Phoebe (Ro 16:1) and Apphia (Phm 1:2) he was not using the words lightly.

The most powerful description of the way Paul entered into a leadership relationship is found in two metaphors he chooses in 1 Thessalonians 2. Keep in mind as you read this passage that Paul's leadership was under attack. He could have come out fighting, since he had the Lord's appointment and divine commission, as well as the education and experience. He could have come to Thessalonica with power and strongly put people in their place. He did not choose this common approach. Instead he employed God's grace (uncommon love), keeping his eyes on his purpose and calling.

The Leader as a "Caring Mother"

> We were gentle among you, like a mother caring for her little children. We loved you so much that we were delighted to share with you not only the gospel of God but our lives as well, because you had become so dear to us. Surely you remember, brothers, our toil and hardship; we worked night and day ...
>
> —1Th 2:7-9

The reference in the Greek language is to a nursing mother[4] gently sharing the food of life with her child. This is a beautiful picture that implies a special effort to protect and to provide for the child's every need, even to the extent of great sacrifice. What the nursing mother has to provide is the nourishment necessary for life. Paul's desire was to share the "Bread of Life" and the "Living Water" with all who are a part of the Kingdom.

A key word in Paul's metaphor is gentleness. Have you ever seen a mother yell at her child and command that child to come and nurse? Whether a child is quiet and cuddling or crying and fussing, you can observe the same gentle spirit in a mother as she brings the child to her breast. A fussing child often does not know why it is feeling upset and cannot voice the reason. The same is true with immature Christians. They do not always know what they need or why they are disturbed by life's choices. Therefore, the Kingdom Leader gently brings them to the word of God that nourishes and brings growth. Mothers realize the day will come when the child will no longer need to come to her breast for nourishment. Similarly, leaders must realize that with proper instruction, the growing Christian will someday be feeding others.

Seldom will you see a mother who is disturbed by her child's desire for nourishment. There is a deep desire to provide. I have had church people call me late at night and say, "I have a question that is bothering me." That does not upset me. My ministry is one of teaching and building people. If the opportunity to teach and build comes late at night, then you pull that person to you to share God's Word. Paul says that he was *delighted* to share with them (1Th 2:8). There is no greater delight for a Kingdom Leader than to see healthy, growing followers.

Like a nursing mother, Paul speaks of his toil and hardship, day and night (1Th 2:9). All around the world we find stories of mothers who have willingly sacrificed their needs or their very lives in order to care for their children. One of the most disturbing stories I have heard was reported by the family that experienced it. A member of their family was killed in an automobile accident that happened during the night in front of the church the family attended. A family member rushed to the pastor's door to report what happened. The pastor told the family to call him in the morning when he was in his office and then shut the door. A pastor from another denomination stopped for the accident and offered his assistance. He went to the hospital with the family and spent the night with them. Can you guess to which congregation that family belongs today? Can you imagine a nursing mother telling her crying child that she will provide care in the morning?

I once had a student in a university class stand up and shout, "Weakness, weakness, I cannot stand this sugar-coated form of leadership." This man was very mistaken, because gentleness is never weak. Gentleness is the strong self-sacrificing spirit that makes heroes and martyrs. It takes more power to restrain an outburst of temper than to let it go. It takes more power to hold one's tongue than to speak words in anger. It takes more power to love a child than to berate a child. It takes more power to be a leader than to be a dictator.

The Leader as an "Encouraging Father"

> For you know that we dealt with each of you as a father deals with his own children, encouraging, comforting and urging you to live lives worthy of God, who calls you into his kingdom and glory.
> —1Th 2:11-12

When I was a child, I was very involved in my school's sports teams. Every week we would play teams from other schools, and I could always count on my father being at the game. My father had a very loud voice and there were times I was a little embarrassed when he shouted out words of encouragement to me, but I was never sorry he was there giving his support. His presence and words are still vivid in my mind forty years later.

My father's example has always played a strong part in my understanding of this picture of Paul's ministry. The Greek word Paul uses here is the same word that describes the ministry of the Holy Spirit—the One who comes alongside. Whereas my father shouted from the stands, Paul's picture is of a father running beside his son in the tough miles of a marathon, saying, "You can do it, son. Come on, just a little more and you will be there."

Probably one of the most gripping stories of what Paul is picturing took place in the 1992 Olympics in Madrid, Spain. Derek Redmond, a runner from Great Britain, had qualified for the final race. After the race began he felt a pain in his leg and he fell to the ground in pain. With excruciating pain, he attempted to complete his race. His father came running out of the crowd, put Derek's arm over his shoulders and the two of them finished the race together.

The picture of a leader as a father is frequently used in Scripture. However, it is always used in the same context as Paul's choice in 1 Thessalonians. It is never used in the sense of a father's authority over his family. "Whenever Jesus uses the term 'father' he is speaking either of literal biological descent, or of God as Father, but never of one disciple in relationship to another."[5] Paul uses *father* to describe his relationship to Timothy (Php 2:22). It is important to note, however, that Paul does not say, "Timothy served me," but rather that he served *with me*. His description of himself as Timothy's father in no way implies an inferior or servant status for the young evangelist. To read his two letters to Timothy and note his references to the young evangelist in other letters, it is clear that Paul's whole purpose in his relationship to Timothy was to build him up, to prepare him for ministry.

As we trace this concept of leadership as fathering, it is important to recognize that Paul never does so in a way that attempts to keep his children weak and dependent. As we have mentioned before, a power-based leader must keep followers weak and dependent because they might eventually overthrow his position. This was never Paul's worry.

One biblical scholar writes,

> We are never to adopt toward a fellow man in the Church the attitude of dependence which a child has towards his father, nor are we to require others to be or to become spiritually dependent on us ... It is ridiculous for one Christian to claim the authority of a father over a fellow Christian and demand his subordination as a child if the two are in reality brothers ... It is, then, the authority of a father over dependent children which is forbidden to us.[6]

I know of no culture that requires a father to make his children dependent on him for a lifetime. In fact fathering has the opposite goal, to build and prepare children to become independent so that they can leave home and successfully build their own. To do that the father has to know the child and encourage growth in all areas. One leadership author claims that leadership is the ability to polish, liberate and enable.[7] That is exactly what Paul was attempting in Thessalonica.

To build a proper concept of leadership a leader needs only to ask the question, "What kind of relationship would I have liked to have with my father?" Or possibly to ask, "What life lessons do I wish my father had taught me?" Answering these questions in light of leadership responsibility can go a long way to helping us understand Paul's heart and what we can accomplish as leaders.

Conclusion

No one, outside of Jesus, had more authority than the Apostle Paul. No Apostle had more qualifications than Paul. He had family status, religious and philosophical education, natural ability and the confidence of his peers. "If anyone else thinks he has reasons to put confidence in the flesh, I have more," Paul wrote in Philippians 3:4. He then confessed, "I consider everything a loss compared to the surpassing greatness of knowing Christ Jesus my Lord" (Php 3:8). Then he added, "Join with others in following my example" (Php 3:17).

From having the "authority to bind" people (Ac 9:14) to having the "authority to build up" people (1Co 10:8), Paul made a total turn in his understanding of leadership. He changed from the marching zealot—who took control of others—to the nursing mother/encouraging father who built people so they might build others (2Ti 2:2).

We, as leaders, must continually evaluate our relationship to those we lead. After encountering our leadership—preaching, counseling or meeting—have they felt our anger or our encouragement? Do they understand what they are to do, or have we only told what they should not do? Have we made them feel weaker or stronger? Have we bound them or built them?

CHAPTER ELEVEN

UNCOMMON COURAGE

My oldest son, Dean Kuest, was scheduled to preach during convocation at Hope International University in Fullerton, California on September 13, 2001—two days after the terrorist attacks on the World Trade Center and the Pentagon. I was touched by his message, and asked him to write it as the final chapter of our leadership study. Dean's sermon came out of his desire to show that the people of Scripture are no different than we are when times call for courage. The same God that encouraged the people in the biblical narrative is the same God who stands ready to provide what we will need.

It is a joy for me to be invited to speak at my alma mater, a school which I love. I know we have experienced some very troubling days and I am sure they are not over. It is times like this that call men and women to courage. And, frankly, sometimes we do not believe we have much to call upon, especially when we compare ourselves to the great men and women of Scripture whose courage we admire so much.

We tend to ascribe super-human characteristics to men and women of faith, but it is not difficult to read between the lines and discover that they trembled with fear just as we do. They doubted just as we doubt. And they failed just as we fail. In our search for uncommon courage we can find clues in the lives of the leaders in Scripture. However, if we are to emulate their courage, we must discover its source.

THE SOURCE OF UNCOMMON COURAGE

There are those who will say that courage is defined as the absence of fear, or at the least, overcoming it to the point where it no longer dictates your life. We hear sayings such as, "Pull yourself up by the boot straps." "Reach down deep inside and you will find it there." "Just do it." As much as we will it, we cannot always get courage to rise.

Americans saw tremendous acts of courage demonstrated by rescue workers as they rushed into the crumbling World Trade Center Towers to save

Uncommon Courage

people trapped by the terrorist attacks on New York City and our Pentagon in Washington, D.C. New York City lost 345 firemen and policemen as those buildings fell. Their commitment to help others compelled them to put their lives on the line. The world has hailed their actions as uncommon courage, and surely it was. However, I believe their acts were motivated by something deeper than just "looking inside themselves." They entered those buildings because they saw a need greater than themselves, and they were committed to answer the call.

As we see a world spinning out of control without the message of God's grace, do we sense a need that is greater than ourselves? Is inner commitment enough to help us grasp the courage needed for a life of faith as we carry out the work of Jesus? Can we find within ourselves the courage to live as strangers in this world (1 Pe 1:3) while people laugh, criticize, or persecute us for our stand? Or, is the source of courage to be found beyond ourselves?

To become the leaders that Christ expects us to be, we must get back to a biblical understanding of courage. To do this, let us examine the courage of four men. These men had to learn to trust a greater source than their own to get them through troubled waters. It is only when we draw from the same source that we can be fully used by God.

My eyes have been opened by the stories of Moses, Joshua, Gideon, Elijah and the many who have come after them. God recorded their stories to teach us. I would like to share with you the one simple message I have identified. It is a message that God has been attempting to communicate to His people from the beginning. It is a message that He whispers in my ear as I search for the uncommon courage to serve Him. It is simply, "It is not about you. It is about Me within you."

At first, this message seems to be lacking power or brilliance. Of course…we all suspected that already. What I have been convicted of is how little the truth of this statement plays out in my life. I would much rather say that I had it within me to do the courageous acts, or to use my lack of it as an excuse for not stepping up in the time of need. However, I take solace in the fact that it took awhile for Moses to understand it as well. Let's jump back in time to Exodus 3 as Moses' curiosity about a burning bush led to a courage-challenging encounter in the very presence of God.

God had a plan for Moses. In spite of his forty-year exile from the land of Egypt, God called upon Moses to return for the purpose of freeing His people from slavery. It was no small order. Egypt was the most powerful nation in the world, and had held power over the Hebrew nation for over 400 years. Now God was calling upon one man to change history. Moses was obviously skeptical. As God disclosed His plan for Moses' confrontation with Pharaoh, we find the Hebrew hero quick with five excuses as to why he could not possibly be the person for the task. God obviously had the wrong man. It is in God's response to Moses' excuses that I first discovered the heart of God's message to us.

Excuse #1: Who Am I?

"Who am I, that I should go to Pharaoh and bring the Israelites out of Egypt?" (Ex 3:11). These words of Moses betray his faulty worldview. "Who am I?" implies that Moses believed it was all about himself. God's answer is much like the whisper of the wind as He says, "I will be with you." This is the place from which confidence is derived. The Creator, the Sustainer, the God who holds all things in the palm of His hand is with me. Without this confidence, courage is impossible. In fact, the rest of Moses' experience with God at the burning bush is about instilling that confidence in him.

Excuse #2: Who Are You?

"Suppose they ask me, 'What is his name?' Then what shall I tell them?" (Ex 3:13). Hear the cynicism in Moses' voice: "Lord, this is going to be a tough one to sell. I will be laughed at if I mention anything about a burning bush speaking to me, so what do you expect me to tell them? I don't even know your name. I'm not sure I know whom I'm talking to." Moses was obviously concerned about the disbelief of his audience. This betrays his own lack of certainty.

Once again God reminded Moses that this had very little to do with Moses and everything to do with God. God says "I AM WHO I AM" is the one who sent you. This name describes God as the One who was, who is, and forever will be. God reminded Moses that, "I am to be remembered" (3:15)." I have watched over you" (3:16). "I have promised to bring you out of your misery" (3:17). "I will stretch out my hand" (3:20). "I will perform wonders among them" (3:20). "I will make the Egyptians favorably disposed toward My people" (3:21). In other words, God is communicating to Moses that I AM is at work. With that knowledge, Moses can rest. It is all about I AM, the ever present active God, who will do what is needed.

Excuse #3: How Will They Know?

"What if they do not believe me or listen to me and say, 'The Lord did not appear to you?'" (Exodus 4:1). Obviously, Moses was not convinced. Therefore, the Lord performed a demonstration of His power to once again illustrate the fact that Moses needed only to rely upon I AM for his ability to complete this task.

Excuse #4: I Am Not Able

"O Lord, I have never been eloquent, neither in the past nor since you have spoken to your servant. I am slow of speech and tongue" (Ex 4:10). God responded by reminding Moses that He had created his mouth, and if He had formed it, He could use it. I am like Moses. I always want to bring everything back to myself. But it is not *me*—my knowledge, my abilities, my position, my strength, or my courage. How many times must my prayers sound like Moses' excuses? All the while God's voice to me speaks,

"It's not about you, it's about Me and My presence with you."

Excuse #5: I Am Not Willing

Finally, Moses blurted out, "O Lord, please send someone else to do it" (Ex 4:13). Moses had run out of excuses. There was nothing he could say to counter what God had to say; therefore, he resorted to desperation. This time, God was less patient. The Scripture says that God's anger burned against Moses. Nevertheless, in His anger, God provided a comfort for Moses. He sent Aaron, Moses' brother, to be his mouthpiece.

I find it interesting that, at the end of Moses' excuses, God relented and provided what Moses thought he needed. When Moses was unable to trust in a God He could not see, God provided a person who represented the very promises to which He had already committed.

Even as Aaron began the trek to find His brother Moses, God was saying, "It is not about you. It is not about Aaron. It is not about any other 'thing' that might make you feel better. It is about Me and My presence with you; however, I will provide for you what your lack of faith requires." Moses was slow to understand. However, he finally obeyed. Through his obedience, Moses became the vehicle through which God was able to demonstrate His might and lead Israel out of slavery. It took awhile, but Moses finally understood.

I soon discovered that the same message God delivered to Moses did not stop in the pages of Exodus. It is intertwined within the stories of all of the great heroes of the faith. Read how Joshua led Israel to the walled city of Jericho (Jos 6). Why would God instruct the nation of Israel to march around the walls seven times and then bring down those walls with only a shout? He wanted the nation of Israel to understand the very same thing that he desired Moses to understand. It is not about you and the strength of your army. It is about Me and My presence with you.

Gideon learned the same lesson (Jdg 6). As the Midianites brought their armies against Israel, Gideon inquired of the Lord what He should do. Gideon communicated an understanding of his own weakness when he asked, "'But Lord, how can I save Israel? My clan is the weakest in Manasseh, and I am the least in my family." The Lord answered, "I will be with you..." (Jdg 6:15). To make matters worse, Midian was joined by the Amalakites, and other eastern people (Jdg 6:33).

Gideon's problem was now three times larger than when it presented itself. This was like the second terrorist plane hitting the World Trade Towers. It was bad at first. Now, it was really a problem beyond one's normal capabilities.

To prove His point to Gideon and Israel, God instructed Gideon in the selection of his undermanned army. The Lord said to Gideon, "In order that Israel may not boast against me that her own strength has saved her, announce now to the people, 'Anyone who trembles with fear may turn back and leave Mount Gilead.' So, twenty-two thousand men left, while ten thousand remained" (Jdg 7:2-3).

God, however, was not through demonstrating His principle to Gideon and the nation of Israel. The Lord said to Gideon, "There are still too many men" (Jdg 7:4). The process of elimination brought the number in Gideon's army to three hundred men—300 against 135,000. What staggering odds. Nevertheless, with that small force, God defeated the combined armies. What did God communicate in this victory? It's not about you; it is about Me and My presence with you.

From Knowledge to Understanding

> "…and if you call out for insight and cry aloud for understanding, and if you look for it as for silver and search for it as for hidden treasure, then you will understand the fear of the Lord and find the knowledge of God. For the Lord gives wisdom, and from His mouth come knowledge and understanding."
> —Pr 2:3-5

Great peace can be found in the knowledge that uncommon courage is not dependent upon us. It is found in the God who dwells within us. Knowing where uncommon courage comes from is one thing; it is quite another to know how to apply it to my life. I do not want to simply know about courage; I want it to overwhelm my life to the point of action. The two enemies of courage are fear and risk. Some have tried to imply that to experience courage is to know no fear and to fear no risk. I do not believe this. The very concept of courage implies fear, for if there were no fear, it would require no courage. The absence of risk implies security, and security requires no courage. God never promises to remove risk. Quite the opposite, God promises that we will be placed at risk if we choose to follow Him. God's message has never changed from that which He spoke to those He calls into service. He never promised Moses that all would be well in Egypt. Instead, He gave him a staff to be used in the presence of challenge. Moses went, knowing that he could call upon "I AM THAT I AM"—the God who is always present and active. "Many times what we want from God is not a mandate that requires our faith, but a guarantee that in reality, faith was never needed."[1]

Matthew chapter 10 tells us that Jesus sent out the disciples to preach. Matthew would have been one of these men. He was to be on his own as a Kingdom Leader for the first time. Can we put ourselves in Matthew's sandals? Can we understand the emotions that must have been swirling in his mind as Jesus commissioned these men to go and spread the news of the Kingdom? Most likely, Matthew was an unskilled orator. He did not have the schooling of the religious leaders of the time. He was a tax collector; the others knew only the family trade. Meeting Jesus changed Matthew's life and He called him to follow. We, like Matthew, have chosen to faithfully follow Jesus, and now He is asking us to leave our comfort zone and trust Him. It is within this scene that Matthew records Jesus' words,

> Be on your guard against men; they will hand you over to the local councils and flog you in their synagogues. On my account you will be brought before governors and kings as witnesses to them and to the Gentiles. But when they arrest you, do not worry about what to say or how to say it. At that time you will be given what to say, for it will not be you speaking, but the Spirit of your Father speaking through you.
> —Mt 10:17-20

This message encompasses the reality of the situation as well as the hope that comes through faith. What Jesus asked for requires uncommon courage. Do you hear His message? Life has no guarantee of ease and comfort. In fact, Jesus assures His disciples that hard times are ahead; yet, in those difficulties He gives assurance. I don't know about you, but I want certain assurances that everything is going to be OK in this life. I would love to believe (as far too many churches in America teach) that God wants to bestow upon me financial blessings and good health in exchange for my undying commitment to Him. I see no examples of this anywhere in Scripture. Instead, I see statements like the one above and Jesus' words found in Jn 16:33. "In this world you will have trouble. But take heart! I have overcome the world."

If we are to truly follow in the footsteps of Christ, fear and risk *will* be a part of our life. This is why courage is so important. We must always remember that in spite of our weakness, He is strong. The assignment is not about us; it is about God's presence within us. God says, "I will bring about My plan through your obedience."

When Jesus concluded the earthly portion of His ministry, He once again spoke with His disciples. We know His words as *The Great Commission*. "Therefore go and make disciples of all nations, baptizing them in the name of the Father and of the Son and of the Holy Spirit, and teaching them to obey everything I have commanded you. And surely I am with you always, to the very end of the age" (Mt 28:19-20). Once again, do you hear His message? It is the same message delivered to Moses, Joshua, and Gideon. No matter what situation we might find ourselves, it is not about us, it is about God's presence within us. He is our strength. He is our power. He is our success.

BUILDING A FOUNDATION FOR COURAGE

Truth leads to love
Love leads to faith
Faith leads to selflessness
Selflessness leads to acts of courage.

There was a foundation of trust that enabled the disciples to take the teachings of Jesus beyond a simple knowledge to a lifestyle that changed the world. It is the same foundation we must build upon in order to live a life of uncommon courage.

Truth Leads Us to Love

Love can be built on many foundations. Many have built love on foundations of falsehoods only to find it crumbling under the weight of their expectations. Time exposes the weakness of the foundation. It is imperative that love be built on truth. Truth does not erode over time. Christ loved us, and as a result, He came to bring truth to us. As the truth is revealed to us about the person of God and the extent of His love for us, we, in turn, love Him back. The truth leads us to love.

Love Leads Us to Faith

When love is built upon truth it leads us into a relationship in which faith is exhibited. Faith is not simply a belief in something. Belief is static, empty, and useless unless it is accompanied by action. James, the brother of Jesus, tells us that very fact. "In the same way, faith by itself, if it is not accompanied by action, is dead" (Jas 1:17). Think about the context of his words. James watched Jesus grow up as his half-brother. Yet, James did not believe the truth of Jesus' claims. In fact, according to Scripture,

Jesus was most likely a source of great embarrassment for James and his family. At one point, as Jesus was teaching in his hometown, His family came to get him—to take Him away due to the commotion that He was causing (Mt 12:46-50). I am sure that James, being Jesus' brother, loved Jesus. However, that love was not built upon truth. It was love built upon a weak foundation—until Jesus' resurrection from the dead. At that point something clicked for James. He went from being a skeptic to a believer, from a man who loved his brother, to a man who had faith in his brother as the Son of God. Love, built upon the truth, led him to faith.

Faith = Belief + Action. When we place the trust of our life in Christ, our hearts and our lives must follow. Why is this? Because just as love leads us to faith, faith leads us to giving the whole of our lives to the needs and desires of the one who loved us. It is what we call *selflessness*.

Faith Leads to Selflessness

Peter clearly wrote about the action to which faith leads. "To this you were called, because Christ suffered for you, leaving you an example, that you should follow in His steps" (1Pe 2:21). Peter points out that Christ did not suffer for His own good. He did not suffer in order to benefit Himself. He suffered for us because that is the character of true love and it brings glory to His Father. That is what a Good Shepherd does for the sheep. He puts the benefit of His sheep at a higher priority than the benefit of self.

When love is built upon truth, it follows with a faith that is enveloped not just in what we believe, but in our lifestyle. Every thought, every word, every action or lack of action is an act of worship to the God who we believe is the essence of all that is true. This is why Paul explains in Ro 12:1, "Therefore, I urge you, brothers, in view of God's mercy, to offer your bodies as living sacrifices, holy and pleasing to God—this is your spiritual act of worship." We give ourselves to the best interest of the God who has given Himself to us for our best interests. We love because he first loved us. We become selfless because he was selfless first. He is the teacher; we are the students who are to walk in the teacher's steps.

SELFLESSNESS LEADS TO ACTS OF COURAGE

This is where the world most often gets it wrong. Believing that courage rises from within us, they misidentify its source. Uncommon courage is not internal; it has an external source. It comes from a knowledge that God has acted and continues to act on our behalf. Therefore, we are compelled to act upon His. Believing that God will act is the beginning of the uncommon courage found in Moses, Gideon, Matthew, Paul and thousands of other saints throughout history.

Courage is manifested when, in the face of need, we acknowledge the truth of God's love for His people. Accepting this truth, our embrace of God's love overcomes our individual story and security. Our worldview trusts God to act, thus allowing us to become a part of God's interaction with mankind. God becomes more important than anything that could happen to me in this life, knowing that God transcends this life, and we take His hand to share with him in that transcendence. There is a bigger story than what is happening within each of our personal contexts, and that leads us to selflessness. As Erwin McManus said, "Courage is not the absence of fear but the absence of self."[2]

Two Reminders

As we conclude our look at courage, two stories from Scripture remind us that we must never forget the source of this uncommon courage. As we begin to practice it in our lives we will find the joy of discovering how God will come through in spite of our weakness. It is exhilarating to be transformed and used by God.

We must never forget the source of our strength. We are tempted to believe that it was our talent, rather than His power, which enabled God to work. We are all prone to take credit for anything good that might come from our efforts. Such is the case of King Uzziah (II Ch 26). Uzziah did what was right in the eyes of the Lord. As long as he sought the Lord, God gave him success (26:5). Scripture then lists the extent of His success, which was great both in battle and in the development of Judah. The historian, however, gives us this sad postscript to the life of Uzziah, "But after Uzziah became powerful, his pride led to his downfall. He was unfaithful to the Lord his God…" (26:16). Uzziah forgot that it was not about him. He looked around and began to believe that it was he who had built Israel and who had won the battles in victory. We also forget. We all need reminders.

Second, even in victory, I am still tempted to forget that God stands with me when the next trial of faith visits me. I marvel at Elijah. The faith, courage and boldness that it took to stand upon Mount Carmel and challenge the prophets of Baal are foreign to my life. This was a duel to the death and Elijah knew it. However, he also understood that this contest was not about him, but it was about God in him. In honor of Elijah's faith and courage, God came through in a mighty way. He sent a ball of fire from the sky to consume a water-saturated altar.

God used the courage and faith of Elijah to convince the people that He is who He says He is; yet, only days later, we find Elijah in hiding. Queen Jezebel heard of the defeat of "her" prophets and she was not too happy. She put a price on Elijah's head. In spite of God's mighty work just days before, Elijah saw that his survival was dependent upon himself and not upon the Lord. He ran away and hid in a cave.

I, for one, am encouraged by Elijah's failure. I identify with his weakness more than I identify with his strength. I am also buoyed by God's response to Elijah. God met Elijah in his weakness and failure. He met him, not in the mighty fireball from the sky, nor in a mighty storm. Instead, God spoke to him in quietness, in a still small voice. God whispered to Elijah, reminding him once more that it was not about him, but about God's presence with him. He held Elijah's life in His hand. Today, I choose to hold onto the same hand that reached out to Elijah. I want to be used in His great plan for the nations. I pray that this is the desire of each one who reads these pages. However, to do so, we must remember,

"Uncommon Courage is not about us…it's about God in us!"

EPILOGUE

One Final Fatal Word

God has clearly presented what He desires in Kingdom Leadership. He set the example in the Garden. He guided the lives of His leaders and authors. His son modeled the standard of measurement. In fact, Jesus *is* that standard of measurement. His principles are not accepted as common practice in many circles. However, if we are to be effective in His Kingdom we must be guided by His higher thinking.

However, I must give final caution before we end. The most dangerous word in the study of biblical leadership is, "But ..." Whenever we speak this word we are usually saying, "I understand what the Bible says, *but* I don't think it applies to me or my situation." We believe we have found an exception to biblical principle. Usually what it means is that, "I don't want to do it that way; therefore, I am going to claim that the Bible really doesn't mean what I am reading." This is the same deception that took place in the Garden of Eden. God's children were convinced that they knew better than their Creator did. Their bite into the fruit began the decline of man's thinking into what we know today as *common sense*.

In a university class of ministerial students, I asked the students to tell me what "The Beatitudes" (Mt 5:3-12) and the "Fruit of the Spirit" (Gal 5:22-23) had to say about leadership. One young man replied, "But professor, those are not leadership Scriptures." I asked the young man, "Are you saying that these Scriptures apply to some places in your life but not every place?" He answered, "No, that's not what I am trying to say, but …" Later the young man agreed that he must allow Scripture to speak to every part of his life.

In most question and answer periods during leadership seminars, the word "but" always seems to creep into the session. It usually takes the conversation to common thinking. "But," the questioner will say, "that doesn't *seem* right because I know someone who *seems* successful, and he is not doing what you say." Remember, God's definition of success is different from the world's. His ways are higher than the common ways; they are higher than those that seem right. We must be very careful that we do not

Epilogue

allow our view of leadership in the Kingdom of God to be misaligned by what seems right. After all, the Apostle Paul, who practiced common principles before his conversion warns us, "See to it that no one takes you captive through hollow and deceptive philosophy, which depends on human tradition and the basic principles of this world rather than on Christ" (Col 2:8).

I challenge the readers of this book to be willing to lift their eyes above the common and find the joy of Kingdom Leadership as love grows among people who have learned to serve. In doing so we will see lives changed.

APPENDIX A

A COMPARISON OF PLATO'S PHILOSOPHY VS. THEOLOGY REVEALED THROUGH MOSES

MOSES – Hebrew Worldview	PLATO – Greek Worldview
One God -- Jehovah	Many gods -- Zeus, the head
God is ultimate reality	Nature is ultimate reality
God created nature	Nature defines god
Man has *free will*	Man controlled by *fate*
Love based "God is love . . ." "For God so loved . . ."	**Power based** Zeus overthrew his father, Cronus Cronus had defeated the Titans
Ultimate Power = Restraint of power	Ultimate power = control
Serve	**Be Served** [1]
See to the needs of others	Aloof from needs of others
Functions by *covenant* -- "for the others' good"	Functions by *command* -- "for the leader's good" [2]
Success = matured people	Success = number of servants
God's ultimate goal - "a people to bless"	**Deity's ultimate goal - "a people to use"**

[1] Plato's conversation between Socrates and Gorgias in *The Gorgias*.

Gorgias - That good, Socrates, which is truly the greatest, being that which gives to men freedom in their own persons, and to individuals the power of ruling over others in their several states.

Socrates - And the same holds of the relation of rhetoric to all the other arts; the rhetorician need not know the truth about things; he has only to discover some way of persuading the ignorant that he has more knowledge than those who know.

Plato. *The Gorgias*. Trans. Benjamin Jowett. Retrieved September 17, 2002 from Internet Classics Archive, http://classics.mit.edu/Plato/gorgias.html (October 15, 2001).

[2] "Plato's ideal state is an aristocracy, a Greek word which means "rule by the best." The lower end of human society, which, as far as Plato is concerned, consists of an overwhelming majority of people in a state, he calls the "producers," since they are most suited for productive work. The middle section of society, a smaller but still large number of people, make up the army and the police and are called "Auxiliaries." The best and the brightest, a very small and rarefied group, are those who are in complete control of the state permanently; Plato calls these people "Guardians." In the ideal state, "courage" characterizes the Auxiliaries; "wisdom" displays itself in the lives and government of the Guardians. A state may be said to have "temperance" if the Auxiliaries obey the Guardians in all things and the Producers obey the Auxiliaries and Guardians in all things."

Richard Hooker. Retrieved May 11, 2002 from
http://www.wsu.edu: 8080/~dee/GREECE/ PLATO.HTM (1996).

APPENDIX B

LEADERSHIP STYLES CHART

LEADERSHIP STYLES

This chart is designed to compare and contrast the foundational thinking of the two leadership bases that are presented in this book.

Servant Based	Power Based
Transformational Leadership Ford, Leighton: *Transforming Leadership.* Burns, James M: *Leadership*	**Transactional Leadership** Defined by James M. Burns, but not advocated by him.
Brings *positive* change Accept change is a participative *process* Works on an awareness of *felt needs* Leads by vision and goal	Resists any change If change must happen, it is viewed as an *exchange process* Leads by bargaining, "What is in it for me?" "What will I get if I . . . ?"
The Builder Covenantal Leadership DePree, Max: *Leadership Is an Art*	**The User**
Works for what is best for the people Emphasizes and participates in the training process Establishes agreements with others that will promote the best for leaders and those led.	Works to control thoughts and actions Withholds information Uses rules and policies to builds fences around people's free thought.
The Involved Leader Incarnational Leadership McKinna, David: *Grace to Lead, Power to Follow*	**The Isolated Leadership**
Visits among the people Learns ideas, needs and hopes of people Based on John 1:14 "Our Incarnational *being* is to embody the Spirit of Christ; our Incarnational *doing* is to empower His people." McKinna, p. 16	Establishes a leadership location away from the people and works behind a closed door. Communicates through *representatives*
The Empowering Leader Mission-Oriented Leadership Blanchard, Kenneth: *Leadership by the Book.*	**The Controlling Leader** Command-Oriented Leadership

Philosophy of German military leadership for over 150 years.
Trusts people with the mission
The goal is *empowerment*
   Empower leaders with purpose of the mission and allow them to make decisions without confirmation of HQ's
	Philosophy of most military leadership defeated by Germany in 150 years.
	Does not trust people with decision making
	The goal is *control*
	   Requires leaders to consult HQ's before any change in *orders* are allowed

Motivational Leadership Hybels, Bill. *Courageous Leadership*	**Manipulative Leadership**
People are encouraged to learn and grow in abilities People are encouraged toward goals that will fulfill common needs.	People are driven toward goals that fulfill needs of those in power. Rewards are given for those who comply with the leader's desires.

Appendix B: Leadership Styles Chart

'I have not found any modern leadership authors who outwardly promote these power-based styles (as did Plato and Machiavelli). The styles on the right side of this chart are taken from my personal experiences and the many stories I hear about leaders from the students who attend classes through the School of Professional Studies at Hope International University in Fullerton, CA. In my years as an Associate Adjunct Professor, the majority of the working students have reported that the power-based side of this comparison best described their employer or immediate superior.

APPENDIX C

TRANSLATION COMPARISONS OF WORDS USED FOR LEADERSHIP[1]

APPENDIX C
TRANSLATION COMPARISONS OF WORDS USED FOR LEADERSHIP

Proistemi
"To stand before while caring for those being led" (Bromiley, p. 939)

Scripture	English (NKJV)	English (NIV)	Thai	Lao	Hmong (White)	Hmong (Blue)	Lisu	Kachin	Akah	Burmese	Chinese
Romans 12:8	He who leads	Leadership	He who controls, grabs, governs	The one who has the power	The one who leads	The Big One	The one who rules with wisdom	Those who control with mercy	Those who lead	Rule intentionally	Serve aggressively
1 Thessalonians 5:12	Who are over you	Who are over you	He who controls...	Appointed leader	Those who look after	Those who look after	Those who lead you	Those who control – govern	Those who look after	Control/ Rule	Clear (gardening)
1 Timothy 5:17	Elders who rule	The elders who direct the affairs	He who controls...	The older Person	Respected ones	Those who look after	Respected Ones – Completed people	Honorable People	Older people	Good ruler	Person who cares for
1 Timothy 3:4,5,12	Manage	Manage	Able to conquer 12 – command	Leads his family 12 – helps	Rules 12 – trains	Presses/ rules 12 – trains	Rules (political)	Who controls 12 – Points the way	Who controls	Able to rule	Takes care of

Hegeomai or Progeomai
"Authority based on character and people's esteem; to give preference" (Bromiley, p.303)

Scripture	English (NKJV)	English (NIV)	Thai	Lao	Hmong (White)	Hmong (Blue)	Lisu	Kachin	Akah	Burmese	Chinese
Romans 12:10	Giving preference	Honor one another	Honor, give preference	Be aggressive in giving honor	Honor seriously	Honor over oneself	Respect	Honor	Consider higher		
Hebrews 13:7,17,24	Those who rule	Your leaders	"The head & the face" Commander	The Leaders	The Leaders	"The First" Number 1	The leaders	Those in front - leaders	The who are the head/ leaders	Those who rule	Those who lead

Episkeptomai or Episkopeo
"To look upon". "To care for" – "The idea of concern is present" (Bromiley, p. 245)

Scripture	English (NKJV)	English (NIV)	Thai	Lao	Hmong (White)	Hmong (Blue)	Lisu	Kachin	Akah	Burmese	Chinese
Acts 20:28	Overseers	Overseers			See Visit	See Visit		One who looks after	Look, See, Care		
1 Peter 5:2-3	Serving as overseers	Serving as overseers			See Visit	See Visit		Nurtures	Nurtures, Takes care of		

The translations in this study are <u>not</u> by linguists, rather by pastors and church leaders reading the Bible in their heart language.

Appendix C: Translation Comparisons of Words Used for Leadership

APPENDIX C
TRANSLATION COMPARISONS OF WORDS USED FOR LEADERSHIP[1]

Scripture	English (NKJV)	English (NIV)	German[2]	Kamba Kikamba	Portuguese	Spanish Reina-Valera	Spanish NVI	German Unity Bible	German Luther
Proistemi — "To stand before while caring for those being led" (Bromiley, p. 939)									
Romans 12:8	He who leads	Leadership	To Lead	One who lays down the rules	Exercise leadership	Those who preside	Who guide with care	Executive	Ruler
1 Thessalonians 5:12	Who are over you	Who are over you	To Lead	The ones who are over you	Exercise leadership	Those who preside	Those who work hard	Executive	Head-master
1 Timothy 5:17	Elders who rule	The elders who direct the affairs	To Lead	Elders who rule well	Those who show spiritual authority	Elders who rule well	Elders who rule well		
1 Timothy 3:4,5,12	Manage	Manage	To Lead	Those who manage well	Govern well	Govern	Govern	4 - Good father 5 - Head-master	Head-master
Hegeomai or Progeomai — "Authority based on character and people's esteem, to give preference" (Bromiley, p. 303)									
Romans 12:10	Giving preference	Honor one another	To Take the Lead	Give preference	Give honor	Give preference	Respecting & honoring one another		
Hebrews 13:7,17,24	Those who rule	Your leaders	Those who lead or guide	Those above you	Your leaders	Pastors	Those in charge	Executives	Teachers
Episkeptomai or Episkopeo — "To look upon"... "To care for" — The idea of concern is present" (Bromiley, p. 245)									
Acts 20:28	Overseers	Overseers	Oversee, Supervise	Shepherds Overseers		Pastors	Those who lead sheep	Shepherd	Shepherd
1 Peter 5:2-3	Serving as overseers	Serving as overseers	Serving as caretakers	As Shepherds Overseers	Position of organizational hierarchy	Serving and being example to others	Caring and being example to others		

[1] The translations in this study are not by linguists, rather by pastors and church leaders reading the Bible in their heart language.

[2] According to the pastors who shared in this translation, "The German always has the sense of responsibility."

APPENDIX D

A NEW TESTAMENT WORD STUDY LEADERSHIP & AUTHORITY

APPENDIX D

A NEW TESTAMENT WORD STUDY
LEADERSHIP & AUTHORITY

New Testament Words for *Leadership*

Greek Word	Type	Description	Scripture	Notes
Proisteme	Caring Leadership	The combination of leading and caring	Romans 12:8	Gift of Leadership
			1 Thessalonians 5:12 1 Timothy 5:17	The responsibility of leadership
			1 Timothy 3:4,5,12	Deacons to be heads of their household but "with an emphasis on care."
Hegeomai Proegeomai	Character Leadership	To Esteem	Hebrews 13:7, 17, 24 Romans 12:10	Authority based in a person's character and people's esteem "to give preference"
		To Think	Matthew 2:6	God's "Ruler" will be the shepherd of His people
		To Rule	Luke 22:26	In God's Kingdom, the one who "rules" will be like the one who serves
		To Lead	Philippians 2:3 & 6	"Think of others' better than yourself"
Dokeo	Character Leadership	To Think, To Believe Be of Good Reputation	Mark 10:42; Galatians 2:2	Paul spoke to those who seemed to be leaders ("those of good reputation")
Exago	Person of Influence	To Lead Out	Matthew 8:23	Jesus led the blind man out
			Acts 5:19; 12:17	Peter led out from jail
			Acts 7:36; Hebrews 8:9	God led Israel out of Egypt
Protos	Servant Leadership	Foremost First - Beginning Chief	Matthew 19:30; 20:27 Mark 9:35; 10:31&44 Luke 13:30	"The first will be last and the last will be first" "Whoever wants to be first must be a slave of all."
			1 Timothy 1:15	Paul was the worst (foremost) among sinners
			Revelation 1:17; 22:13	Jesus is "the First and the Last"
Hodegeo Hodegos	Guiding Leadership	To Show the Way To Guide To Lead	Matthew 15:14; 23:16, 24	"If the blind leads the blind..." Pharisees as "blind guides"
			John 16:13	Holy Spirit will guide into truth
			Acts 8:31	Ethiopian Eunuch — "How can I understand unless someone "explains" (guides) me?"

Appendix D: A New Testament Word Study
Leadership & Authority

APPENDIX D

A NEW TESTAMENT WORD STUDY
LEADERSHIP & AUTHORITY

Guiding & Shepherding

Greek Word	Type	Description	Scripture	Notes
kubernē-ósis	Directing the Course	Helmsman, Ship's Pilot	1 Corinthians 12:28	"If one is gifted with leading, let him lead"
Poimaino Poimen	Shepherding	To Tend (as a shepherd) To Feed To Rule A Shepherd A Pastor	Matthew 2:6	From Bethlehem, a ruler who will shepherd God's people
			John 10:11-18 (Ps 23; Is. 40:10-11; Ez. 34:11-16)	Descriptions of a "Good Shepherd"
			John 21:16	Jesus to Peter – "Take care of my sheep."
			Acts 20:28; 1 Peter 5:2-4	Be shepherds of God's flock
			Ephesians 4:11-13	The purpose of "shepherding" – prepare, build, unite, and teach for maturity
			Jude 1:12 (Ezekiel 34:1-10)	God's anger with self-serving shepherds
			Revelation 2:27; 12:5	How God's Son will "rule"

New Testament Words for Authority

Greek Word	Type	Description	Scripture	Notes
Exousia	Appointed Authority	Authority conferred by a higher authority	Luke 4:6	Authority Satan offered Jesus
			Mark 11:28-29	Authority for which the Jewish leaders demanded a source
			Matthew 28:18	The authority Jesus claimed at Ascension
Kurieuo	Assumed Authority	To rule To lord over	Romans 14:9	Authority that results from inheritance, power struggle or appointment
Archo	Absolute Authority	To Dominate To rule To Be First	Romans 15:12	Root of Jesse to reign over Gentiles
			Revelation 1:8, 21:6, 22:19	Jesus Alpha & Omega
			Ephesians 1:21; Colossians 2:10	Jesus has authority over all authority
			Revelation 17:14, 19:16	King of Kings, Lord of Lords

APPENDIX D

A NEW TESTAMENT WORD STUDY
LEADERSHIP & AUTHORITY

Words of Leadership Service

Greek Word	Type	Description	Scripture	Notes
Episkopos	Caring Leadership	Overseer, Watcher Protector "Used only for leaders of settled congregations" p. 248	1 Peter 2:25	Jesus – "The shepherd and episkopos of your souls"
			Acts 20:28	Overseers to be shepherds
			Philippians 1:1	Paul writes to the saints, overseers and deacons"
			1 Timothy 3:2, Titus 1:7	Qualifications for an overseers
Presbuteros	Wise Leadership	Older, Bearer of tradition Paul refers to their function more than their office, their ministry more than their status. p. 932	Acts 11:30	Recipients of the collection taken for Judean Christians
			Acts 14:23	Elders ordained in every church
			Acts 15	Elders hear differences in opinions about Gentiles and make decision
			James 5:14	Elders to pray for the sick
			1 Timothy 5:17, 19	The elders are to lead, be eligible for pay and protected from accusations.
Diaconos	Serving Leadership	Verb, *diakoneo* = to wait at table, to care for, to serve p. 152	John 2:5, 9	Servants at the wedding feast
			Matthew 22:26, Mark 10:43	To become great one must be a *servant*
			John 12:26	Followers of Christ are *servants*
			Romans 13:4	Civil authorities are servants of God
			Romans 15:8	Jesus is a servant to the Jews
			Romans 16:1	Phoebe is a servant of the Church
			2 Corinthians 3:6; Colossians 1:23, 25	Paul is a servant of the New Testament
			2 Corinthians 3:6; 6:4; 11:15, 25; Galatians 2:17; Ephesians 3:17; 6:21; Colossians 1:7, 23,25; 4:7; 1 Thessalonians 3:2; 1 Timothy 4:6	In each of these references the King James Version translates *diakonos* as *minister*

[1] All definitions are from *Theological Dictionary of the New Testament.* Gerhard Kittel & Gerhard Friedrich, ed. Geoffrey W. Bromiley, Translator. Abridged in One Volume. (New York: William B. Eerdmans' Publishing Co. 1985).

APPENDIX E

DESCENDING TO SERVE

We begin to see a pattern in Jesus' example and teaching about the attitude of leadership. This chart will trace the consistency of his principle of "Descending to Serve."

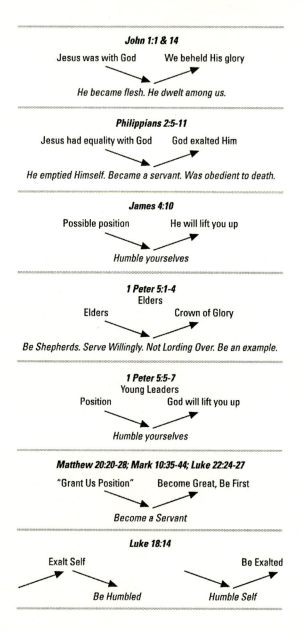

Appendix E
Descending to Serve

Comparison of Leadership Philosophies	
Servant-Based Thinking **Philippians 2:5-11**	**Power-Based Thinking** **Isaiah 14:11-15**
Position is not important 2:6	Pomp (show of importance) 14:11-12
Made himself nothing 2:7a	Self-importance – "I will be at the top" 14:13a
Became a humble servant 2:7b-8a	Power – "I will be in charge" 14:13b
Was obedient 2:8b	Authority – "I will be like God" 14:14
God's Response	
Exalted Him to highest position 2:9-11	Cast him down to the pit 14:15

SOURCE LIST

American Heritage® Talking Dictionary, Hirsch, E.D. Jr, Kent, Joseph F. and Trefil, , John eds., Third Edition CD-ROM. Cambridge, MA: Softkey International, Inc., 1994.

Arndt, William F. & Gingrich, F. Wilbur. *A Greek-English Lexicon of the New Testament and Other Early Christian Literature.* Grand Rapids: Zondervan, 1963.

Barclay, William. *A New Testament Wordbook.* New York: Harper & Row, n.d.

Bennett, David W. *Metaphors of Ministry: Biblical Images for Leaders and Followers.* Grand Rapids: Baker Book House, Paternoster Press, 1993.

Bromiley, Geoffrey.. *Theological Dictionary of the New Testament.* Kittel, Gerhard & Friedrich, Gerhard, ed. Bromiley, Geoffrey, trans Abridged in One Volume. Grand Rapids: Eerdmans, 1985.

Brown, Driver & Briggs. *Brown-Driver-Briggs Hebrew Definitions*. in QuickVerse: Expanded Seventh Version CD-ROM, version 7. Omaha: Parson's Technology, nd.

Burns, James MacGregor. *Leadership*. New York: Colophon Books, Harper & Row, 1979.

Butt, Howard. *The Velvet-Covered Brick: Christian Leadership in an Age of Rebellion*. New York: Harper & Row, 1973.

Carpiceci, Alberto C. *Art and History of Egypt: 5000 Years of Civilization*. Firenze: Casa Editrice Bonechi, 1999.

Clinton, J. Robert. *The Making of a Leader: Recognizing the Lessons and Stages of Leadership Development*. Colorado Springs: NavPress, A Ministry of Navigators, 1988.

Covey, Stephen C. *The Seven Habits of Highly Effective People: Powerful Lessons in Personal Change*. New York: A Fireside Book, Published by Simon & Schuster, 1990.

DePree, Max. *Leadership Is An Art*, Max DePree. New York: A Dell Trade Paperback, published by Dell, 1989.

Edersheim, Alfred. *The Life and Time of Jesus the Messiah*, Book III, "From the Jordan to the Mount of Transfiguration." Grand Rapids: Eerdmans, 1976.

Edersheim, Alfred. *The Life and Time of Jesus the Messiah*, Book V, "The Cross and the Crown." Grand Rapids: Wm. B. Eerdmans Publishing, 1976.

Greenleaf, Robert K. *Servant Leadership: A Journey into the Nature of Legitimate Power and Greatness.* New York, NY: Paulist Press, 1984.

Hagberg, Janet O. *Real Power: Stages of Personal Power in Organizations.* Minneapolis: Winston Press, 1984.

Hian, Chua Wee. *The Making of a Leader: A Guidebook for Present and Future Leaders* Colorado Springs, CO: InterVarsity Press, 1987.

Hooker, Richard. "Plato." Updated June 6, 1999. Washington State University: World Civilizations. http://www.wsu.edu:8080/~dee/GREECE/PLATO.HTM (1996). Accessed May 11, 2002.

Killinger, John. *Fundamentals of Preaching.* Minneapolis: Fortress Press, 1985.

Latourette, Kenneth Scott. *A History of Christianity, vol. 1: Beginnings to 1500.* San Francisco: Harper, 1975.

Lyles, Dick. *Winning Ways: Four Secrets for Getting Great Results by Working Well with People.* New York: G. Putnam's Sons, 2000.

Machiavelli, Niccolo di Bernardo. "The Prince." *The Portable Machiavelli*, Bondanella, Peter & Musa, Mark, translator and editors. New York: Penguin Books, Viking Penguin Inc., 1979.

Maxwell, John C. *The 21 Irrefutable Laws of Leadership: Follow Them and People Will* Follow You. Nashville: Thomas Nelson, 1998.

McKenna, David L. *Power to Follow Grace to Lead: Strategy for the Future of Christian* Leadership. Dallas: Word, 1989.

McManus, Erwin R. *An Unstoppable Force: Daring To Become the Church God Had in Mind*. Loveland: Group Publishing, 2001.

Nouwen, Henri. *In the Name of Jesus: Reflections on Christian Leadership*. New York: Crossroad, 1989.

Passmore, John. "Perfectibility." Posed December 17, 2003. On Line Library of Literature, Liberty Fund, Inc. <u>http://oll.libertyfund.org/Texts/LFBooks/</u>Passmore0198/Perfectibility/PDFs/0092_Pt03_Chap02.pdf. Accessed May 10, 2004.

Plato. *The Gorgias*. Posted October 15, Trans. Benjamin Jowett. Internet Classics Archives, <u>http://classics.mit.edu/Plato/gorgias.html.</u> Accessed September 17, 2002.

Oxford Dictionary of Current English. <u>http://www.askoxford.com/dictionaries/</u>compact_oed/?view=uk (nd). Accessed November 10, 20.

Rinehart, Stacy T. *Upside Down: The Paradox of Servant Leadership*. Colorado Springs: NavPress, 1998.

Ross, Kelly. "Plato's Republic." Posted July 6, 1996. *The Proceedings of the Friesian School, Fourth Series.* <u>http://www.friesian.com/ plato.htm.</u> Accessed May 11, 2003.

Shelley, Bruce. *Church History in Plain Language*. Waco: Word, 1982.

Smith, Mont W. *What the Bible Says About Covenant*. Joplin: College Press, 1981.

Stott, John. *The Preacher's Portrait*, London: Tyndale House, 1961.

Vincent, Marvin R. *Vincent's Word Pictures, Vol. II, "The Writings Of John: The Gospel, The Epistles, The Apocalypse."* Hiawatha: Parsons Technology, Inc., nd.

White, John. *Excellence in Leadership: Reaching Goals with Prayer, Courage and Determination.* Downers Grove: InterVarsity Press, 1986.

Yukl, Gary A. *Leadership in Organizations.* Englewood Cliffs: Prentice-Hall, 1981.

ENDNOTES

Chapter One
UNCOMMON THINKING

[1] Scripture taken from the HOLY BIBLE, NEW INTERNATIONAL VERSION®. COPYRIGHT© 1973, 1978, 1984 by International Bible Society. Used by permission of Zondervan Publishing House. All rights reserved.

[2] John White, *Excellence in Leadership: Reaching Goals with Prayer, Courage and Determination* (Downers Grove: InterVarsity Press, 1986), 36.

[3] John Passmore, "Perfectibility," On Line Library of Literature, Liberty Fund, Inc. Last updated December 17, 2003. http://oll.libertyfund.org/

Texts/LFBooks/Passmore0198/ Perfectibility/ PDFs/0092_Pt03_Chap02.pdf (May 10, 2004).

[4] Plato, "The Gorgias," *Internet Classics Archives*, Trans. Benjamin Jowett., last updated October 15, 2001. http://classics.mit.edu/Plato/gorgias.html (September 17, 2002).

[5] Passmore, 29.

[6] Kelly Ross, *Plato's Republic*, http://www.friesian.com/ plato.htm, last updated July 6, 1996 (May 11, 2003) 5.

[7] Richard Hooker, *Plato*, 1996. http://www.wsu.edu:8080/~dee/GREECE/PLATO.HTM (May 11, 2002).

[8] Appendix A, "A Comparison of Plato's Philosophy To Theology Revealed through Moses," contains a chart that compares the basics of Plato's Greek philosophy to that revealed through Moses, which will be referred to as "Hebrew Thinking." Appendix B, "Leadership Styles," is a comparison of the types of leaders that are found throughout the world. These leadership styles are the result of the philosophical base, or thinking to which a leader is exposed.

[9] *Praus* is the Greek the New Testament for *meek*. In his book, A New Testament Wordbook, William Barclay describes a man who is *meek*. "There is gentleness in *praus* but behind the gentleness there is the strength of steel, for the supreme characteristic of the man who is *praus* is that he is a man who is under perfect control. It is not

a spineless gentleness . . . it is a strength under control" (Barclay. 104).

[10] John Maxwell, *The 21 Irrefutable Laws of Leadership: Follow Them and People Will Follow You* (Nashville: Thomas Nelson, 1998), 107.

[11] Brown, Driver & Briggs, *Brown-Driver-Briggs' Hebrew Definitions* (np), in QuickVerse: Expanded CD-ROM, version 7 (Omaha: Parson's Technology, nd).

[12] The Greek word used by Paul and translated *overseer* literally means "to visit" or "to watch over and show concern for." According to 1 Peter 5:2, leaders, "in tending the flock, watch over it and show a concern for it (on the model of Christ himself as shepherd and *episkopos*) (Bromiley, 1985, p. 245).

[13] Jesus used the Greek noun *paraklete* which has been translated *guide, helper, counselor or aide*. Literally it describes "one who appears in another's behalf, mediator, intercessor, helper" (Arndt, Gingrich, 1963, p. 623).

[14] Robert Greenleaf, *Servant Leadership: A Journey into the Nature of Legitimate Power and Greatness* (New York: Paulist Press, 1984), 13-14.

[15] Stacy Rinehart, *Upside Down: The Paradox of Servant Leadership* (Colorado Springs: NavPress, 1998), 76-77.

CHAPTER TWO
UNCOMMON MEASUREMENTS

[1] Stephen Covey, *The Seven Habits of Highly Effective People: Powerful Lessons in Personal Change,* (New York: A Fireside Book, Published by Simon & Schuster, 1990), 19.

[2] Niccolo di Bernardo Machiavelli, "The Prince" in *The Portable Machiavelli*, translated and edited Peter Bondanella and Mark Musa (New York: Penguin Books, Viking Penguin Inc., 1979), 135.

[3] Patrick Lattore, Lecture, OD 768 – *The Theology, Theory and Practice of Leadership* (Pasadena: Fuller Theological Seminary, Feb. 6, 1991).

[4] Ibid.

[5] Jonathan Adams, "The Company of One," *Power: Who Has it Now,* special report, *Newweek Issues 2004,* http://msnbc.msn.com/id/3606161 (Feb 23, 2005).

[6] Peter Koestenbaum, *Leadership: The Inner Side of Greatness* (San Francisco: Jossey-Bass Publishers, 1991), 92.

[7] Ibid., 102.

[8] Ibid.

CHAPTER THREE UNCOMMON PURPOSE

[1] Henri Nouwen, *In the Name of Jesus: Reflections on Christian Leadership* (New York: Crossroad, 1989), 59.

Endnotes

[2] Quoted in Max DePree, *Leadership Is An Art* (New York: A Dell Trade Paperback, published by Dell Publishing, 1989), 59.

[3] John Killinger, *Fundamentals of Preaching* (Minneapolis: Fortress Press, 1985), 8.

Chapter Four
UNCOMMON PARADIGM

[1] Genesis 14:14 indicates that Abraham had 318 *trained* men. If each man had a wife and children, this would make over 1000 the group he led from Ur of Chaldees to Canaan. When it was necessary to rescue Lot, Abraham's men were already trained to go to battle and they won the battle without the loss of any soldier. These facts show the strength of his leadership.

[2] Chua Wee Hian, *The Making of a Leader: A Guidebook for Present and Future Leaders* (Colorado Springs, CO: InterVarsity Press, 1987), 31.

Chapter Five
UNCOMMON STRATEGY:
COVENANTAL LEADERSHIP

[1] Dick Lyles, *Winning Ways: Four Secrets for Getting Great Results by Working Well with People* (New York: G. Putnam's Sons, 2000), 40.

[2] Covey, 207.

[3] Mont W. Smith, *What the Bible Says About Covenant* (Joplin: College Press, 1986), 6.

[4] Ibid., 9.
[5] Ibid., 23.
[6] Covey, 217.
[7] Ibid., 220.
[8] Ibid., 221.
[9] DePree, 60
[10] Ibid.
[11] Lyles, 41.
[12] Covey, 229.
[13] Ibid, 217.

CHAPTER SIX
UNCOMMON TESTING: HOW LEADERS GROW

[1] E.D. Hirsch, Jr, Joseph F. Kent and John Trefil, eds., "Character", CD-ROM *American Heritage® Talking Dictionary*, Third Edition (Softkey International, Inc., 1994).
[2] Ibid., "Integrity."
[3] J. Robert Clinton, 1998, p. 63.
[4] J. Robert Clinton, *The Making of a Leader: Recognizing the Lessons and Stages of Leadership Development* (Colorado Springs: NavPress, A Ministry of Navigators, 1988), 155.
[5] Howard Butt, *The Velvet-Covered Brick: Christian Leadership in an Age of Rebellion* (New York: Harper & Row, 1973).
[6] Clinton, 156.
[7] Ibid., p. 157.

[8] Janet O. Hagberg, *Real Power: Stages of Personal Power in Organizations* (Minneapolis: Winston Press, 1984), 103.

[9] Ibid.

[10] Ibid., 113.

[11] Clinton, 199.

CHAPTER SEVEN
UNCOMMON AUTHORITY: LEADERS AND POWER

[1] Kenneth Scott Latourette, *A History of Christianity, vol 1: Beginnings to 1500* (San Francisco: Harper, 1975), 112–113.

[2] Paul does give Timothy (1Ti 3:1-13) and Titus (1:6-9) guidelines for choosing people to serve in the church. However, nowhere does he teach the formation of a church board, committee or any other leadership structure. Neither does he dictate that "elders have authority over pastors and deacons" or that "pastors have authority over elders and deacons." This is not to say that leadership structures are bad. However, biblically, one has to realize that any structure is a *form* through which the biblical *function* is to be fulfilled.

[3] Rinehart, 76.

[4] Bruce Shelly, *Church History in Plain Language* (Waco: Word Publishing, 1982), 95.

[5] Latourette, 117.

[6] Rinehart, 78.

[7] See Appendix C – Translation Comparisons of Words Used for Leadership" for a chart of the variety of ways in which translators have interpreted key leadership words into various languages.

[8] A comparison of words translated in Hebrews 13:7, 17 will be discussed later in this chapter. A quick reference for non-Greek scholars can be found by comparing these two verses as found in the King James Version (a power-based translation) and New International Version or New American Standard Versions (servant-based translations).

[9] James MacGregor Burns, *Leadership* (New York: Colophon Books, Harper & Row Publishers, 1979), 12.

[10] Gary Yukl, *Leadership in Organizations* (Englewood Cliffs: Prentice-Hall, Inc., 1981), 65.

[11] Geoffery Bromiley, Gerhard Kittel & Gerhard Friedrich, eds. *Theological Dictionary of the New Testament,* Abridged in One Volume (Grand Rapids: William B. Eerdmans Publishing Co, 1985), 486-487.

[12] Ibid., 81.

[13] David W. Bennett, *Metaphors of Ministry: Biblical Images for Leaders and Followers* (Grand Rapids: Baker Book House, Paternoster Press, 1993), 189.

[14] See Appendix D – "A New Testament Word Study Leadership & Authority" for a listing of words used in the Scriptures to describe leadership in the world and in the Church.

[15] See also, Mark 10:42-45; Luke 22:24-27.
[16] See Acts 9:14; 26:10, 12.
[17] Kenneth Blanchard, Speech, San Diego Leadership Initiative, June 6, 2001.
[18] William F. Arndt & F. Wilbur Gingrich, *A Greek-English Lexicon of the New Testament and Other Early Christian Literature:A translation and adaptiion of Walter Bauer's* Griechisch-Deutsches Wörterbuch zu den Schriften des Neuen Testaments und der übrigen urchistlichen Literatur, fouth edition, (Chicago: The University of Chicago Press, distributed by Zondervan Publishing House, 1963), 690.
[19] Bennett, 58.
[20] Arndt & Gingrich, 690.
[21] Bromiley, 690.
[22] Bennett, 151.
[23] This Latin phrase is used to describe the leadership philosophy of Neferkare, Pharaoh of Egypt from 2130 to 2120 BC (Alberto C. Carpiceci, *Art and History of Egypt: 5000 Years of Civilizatio.* [Firenze: Casa Editrice Bonechi, 1989]. 9). Even though Latin would not have been in existence 2000 years before Christ, Neferkare's uncommon concept of servant-leadership was prominent enough for the historian to apply this phrase.
[24] Greenleaf, 61.
[25] Bennett, 190.
[26] Bromiley, 939.
[27] Greenleaf, 15.
[28] Bromiley, 303.

[29] To translate *hegeomai* in the common understanding of "rule" is to contradict Jesus' instructions to *not lord it over*" (Mt 20:27). It also nullifies Peter's repeating of this instruction in 1 Peter 5:3. Therefore, the translation "rule" does not measure from the Cornerstone.

[30] Arndt & Gingrich, 344.

[31] Bromiley, 303.

[32] Ibid., 178.

[33] Ibid., 152.

[34] Bromiley, 152.

[35] Ibid.

[36] Arndt & Gingrich, 183.

[37] Ibid., 708.

[38] Bennett, 150.

[39] Ibid., 151.

[40] Arndt & Gingrich, 298.

[41] Bromiley, 245.

[42] Bennett, 147.

[43] Ibid., 63.

[44] See Appendix E – "Descending To Serve" for a biblical study on *humility* and *exaltation*.

Chapter Eight

JESUS – AN INCARNATIONAL LEADER

[1]"The Rabbis laid it down as a rule that the learned ought to be most careful in their dress. It was a disgrace if a scholar walked abroad with clouted shoes; to wear dirty clothes deserved death; for 'the glory of God was man, and the glory of man

was his dress.' This held especially true of the Rabbi, whose appearance might otherwise reflect on the theological profession. It was the general rule to eat and drink below (or else according to) a man's means, but to dress and lodge above them. For, in these four things a man's character might be learned: at his cups, in money matters, when he was angry, and by his ragged dress . . . Accordingly, the Rabbis were wont to wear such dress by which they might be distinguished" (Alfred Edersheim, *The Life and Time of Jesus the Messiah*, Book III, *"From the Jordan to the Mount of Transfiguration"* [Grand Rapids: Wm. B. Eerdmans Publishing, 1976], 621).

[2] "They were wont to call Him by the two highest names, of Teacher and Lord, and these designations were rightly His. For the first time He fully accepted and owned the highest homage. How much more, then, must His Service of love, Who was their Teacher and Lord, serve as example of what was due by each to his fellow-disciple and fellow-servant! He, Who really was Lord and Master, had rendered this lowest service to them as an example that, as He had done, so should they do." (Alfred Edersheim, *The Life and Time of Jesus the Messiah*, Book V, *"The Cross and the Crown."* [Grand Rapids: Wm. B. Eerdmans Publishing, 1976], 501).

[3] Ibid., 499.

[4] Machiavelli, 83.

[5] Originally the Greek word *makarios* meant "freedom from cares and worries." It only refers to blessings received by people (i.e. an object could never be *blessed*). In the New Testament it suggests, "the distinctive joy which comes through participation in the divine kingdom" (Bromiley, 548).

[6] Ibid., 506.

[7] *Logos* "is never used in the merely grammatical sense, as simply the *name* of a thing or act, but means a word *as the thing referred to* . . . a word as embodying a conception or idea" (Marvin R. Vincent, *Vincent's Word Pictures*, Vol II, "The Writings Of John: The Gospel, The Epistles, The Apocalypse." CD-ROM QuickVerse Expanded Seventh Edition [Omaha: Parsons Technology, Inc., nd]). The student giving the class report on *logos* claimed that "as a concept" or "idea" the hearer must give a response to their belief in its validity. Thus, the *word* made an *impact* upon the hearer.

Another Greek scholar compares the Greek philosophical concept of *logos* to that of the New Testament. To the Greeks, *logos* was "the principle of harmony that holds all things together" (Bromiley, 507). John reaches the Greek thinker by claiming that "Through [Jesus] all things were made; without him nothing was made that has been made" (Jn 1:3). Thus, as the *logos*, Jesus created all things and holds all things together.

"The Greek *logos* concept is an attempt to master the world [power-based ideology]. It is governed by the human *logos*, which is found again in the cosmic *logos*. To shape life according to the latter is to come to one's true being. In the NT, however, *logos* expresses the specific divine address with which God comes to us here and now with his outside demand and claim ['What will you do with Jesus, My Word, who did not come to be served, but to serve?']" (Bromiley, 507).

[8] David L. McKenna, *Power to Follow Grace to Lead: Strategy for the Future of Christian Leadership.* (Dallas: Word Publishing, 1989), 16.

[9] Ibid., 29.

[10] Ibid., 129.

CHAPTER NINE
DAVID – RULER IN RIGHTEOUSNESS

[1] Brown, Driver & Briggs.

[2] Ibid.

[3] Bromiley, 303.

[4] Ibid., 939.

[5] Nouwen. 58.

CHAPTER TEN
PAUL – BUILDER OF PEOPLE

[1] Paul uses the word *rebuke* 5 times, *admonish* 5 times, *correction* 1, and he uses *warn* 10 times (a

total of 19 times). He uses the *building up* words listed in this sentence a total of 60 times.
2. DePree, xix.
3. Greenleaf, 13-14.
4. The Greek word *trophos* means, "nurse . . . or possibly mother." The verb form, *trophophoreo*, means "to bear up in one's arms as a nurse, i.e. care for someone (tenderly)" (Arndt & Gingrich, 1963, 835).
5. Bennett, 81.
6. John Stott, <u>The Preacher's Portrait</u> (London: Tyndale Press, 1961) np.
7. DePree, 8.

CHAPTER ELEVEN
UNCOMMON COURAGE

1. Erwin R. McManus, *An Unstoppable Force: Daring toBecome the Church God Had in Mind* (Loveland: Group Publishing, 2001), 151. "Used with permission from An Unstoppable Force: Daring to Become the Church God Had in Mind, by Erwin Raphael McManus, published by Group Publishing, PO Box 481, Loveland, CO 80539 www.group.com".
2. From a message delivered by Erwin McManus at the 2004 North American Christian Convention in Phoenix, AZ, July 7, 2004.

APPENDIX C
TRANSLATION COMPARISONS OF WORDS USED FOR LEADERSHIP[1]

[1] The translations in this study are <u>not</u> by linguists, rather by pastors and church leaders reading the Bible in their heart language.

[2] According to the pastors who shared in this translation, "The German always has the sense of responsibility."

To order additional copies of

UNCOMMON LEADERSHIP

Have your credit card ready and call:

1-877-421-READ (7323)

or please visit our web site at
www.pleasantword.com

Also available at:
www.amazon.com
and
www.barnesandnoble.com

Printed in the United States
48714LVS00001B/115-279